I Don It

Keep on Deing
sensitive to
others —

Your friend
John Doyle

INTERPERSONAL SENSITIVITY

John R. Hoyle
Professor of
Educational Administration
Texas A&M University
College Station, TX

and

Harry M. Crenshaw, II
Executive Director,
Secondary Education
Lewisville Independent School District
Lewisville, TX

EYE ON EDUCATION
6 DEPOT WAY WEST, SUITE 106
LARCHMONT, NY 10538
(914) 833–0551
(914) 833–0761 fax

Library of Congress Cataloging-in-Publication Data

```
Hoyle, John.
    Interpersonal sensitivity / John R. Hoyle and Harry M. Crenshaw,
II.
        p.   cm. -- (School leadership library)
    Includes bibliographical references (p. ).
    ISBN 1-883001-29-3
    1. School principals--United States--Attitudes.  2. Interpersonal
relations--United States.  3. School environment--United States.
4. Group relations training--United States.   I. Crenshaw, Harry M.,
1946-   . II. Title.  III. Series.
LB2831.92.U6H67  1997
302'.14--dc20                                         96-32319
                                                         CIP
```

10 9 8 7 6 5 4 3 2 1

Editorial and production services provided by Richard H. Adin Freelance
Editorial Services, 9 Orchard Drive, Gardiner, NY 12525 (914-883-5884)

Published by Eye On Education:

Block Scheduling: A Catalyst for Change in High Schools
by Robert Lynn Canady and Michael D. Rettig

Teaching in the Block
edited by Robert Lynn Canady and Michael D. Rettig

Educational Technology: Best Practices from America's Schools
by William C. Bozeman and Donna J. Baumbach

The Educator's Brief Guide to Computers in the Schools
by Eugene F. Provenzo, Jr.

Handbook of Educational Terms and Applications
by Arthur K. Ellis and Jeffrey T. Fouts

Research on Educational Innovations
by Arthur K. Ellis and Jeffrey T. Fouts

Research on School Restructuring
by Arthur K. Ellis and Jeffrey T. Fouts

Hands-on Leadership Tools for Principals
by Ray Calabrese, Gary Short, and Sally Zepeda

The Principal as Steward
by Jack McCall

The Principal's Edge
by Jack McCall

Leadership: A Relevant and Practical Role for Principals
by Gary M. Crow, L. Joseph Matthews, and Lloyd E. McCleary

Organizational Oversight:
Planning and Scheduling for Effectiveness
by David A. Erlandson, Peggy L. Stark, and Sharon M. Ward

Motivating Others: Creating the Conditions
by David P. Thompson

Oral and Nonverbal Expression
by Ivan Muse

Instruction and the Learning Environment
by James W. Keefe and Harry M. Crenshaw

Interpersonal Sensitivity
by John R. Hoyle and Harry M. Crenshaw

Directory of Innovations in Elementary Schools
by Jane McCarthy and Suzanne Still

The School Portfolio:
A Comprehensive Framework for School Improvement
by Victoria L. Bernhardt

The Administrator's Guide to School-Community Relations
by George E. Pawlas

Innovations in Parent and Family Involvement
by William Rioux and Nancy Berla

The Performance Assessment Handbook
Volume 1: Portfolios and Socratic Seminars
by Bil Johnson

The Performance Assessment Handbook
Volume 2: Performances and Exhibitions
by Bil Johnson

Bringing the NCTM Standards to Life
by Lisa B. Owen and Charles E. Lamb

Mathematics the Write Way
by Marilyn S. Neil

School-to-Work
by Arnold H. Packer and Marion W. Pines

Transforming Education Through Total Quality
Management: A Practitioner's Guide
by Franklin P. Schargel

Quality and Education: Critical Linkages
by Betty L. McCormick

The Educator's Guide to Implementing Outcomes
by William J. Smith

Schools for All Learners: Beyond the Bell Curve
by Renfro C. Manning

FOREWORD

The School Leadership Library was designed to show practicing and aspiring principals what they should know and be able to do to be effective leaders of their schools. The books in this series were written to answer the question, "How can we improve our schools by improving the effectiveness of our principals?"

Success in the principalship, like in other professions, requires mastery of a knowledge and skills base. One of the goals of the National Policy Board for Educational Administration (sponsored by NAESP, NASSP, AASA, ASCD, NCPEA, UCEA, and other professional organizations) was to define and organize that knowledge and skill base. The result of our efforts was the development of a set of 21 "domains," building blocks representing the core understandings and capabilities required of successful principals.

The 21 domains of knowledge and skills are organized under four broad areas: Functional, Programmatic, Interpersonal and Contextual. They are as follows:

FUNCTIONAL DOMAINS
Leadership
Information Collection
Problem Analysis
Judgment
Organizational Oversight
Implementation
Delegation

PROGRAMMATIC DOMAINS
Instruction and the Learning
   Environment
Curriculum Design
Student Guidance and Devel-
   opment
Staff Development
Measurement and Evaluation
Resource Allocation

INTERPERSONAL DOMAINS
Motivating Others
Interpersonal Sensitivity
Oral and Nonverbal Expres-
   sion
Written Expression

CONTEXTUAL DOMAINS
Philosophical and Cultural
   Values
Legal and Regulatory Appli-
   cations
Policy and Political Influences
Public Relations

These domains are not discrete, separate entities. Rather, they evolved only for the purpose of providing manageable descriptions of essential content and practice so as to better understand the entire complex role of the principalship. Because human behavior comes in "bunches" rather than neat packages, they are also overlapping pieces of a complex puzzle. Consider the domains as converging streams of behavior that spill over one another's banks but that all contribute to the total reservoir of knowledge and skills required of today's principals.

The School Leadership Library was established by General Editors David Erlandson and Al Wilson to provide a broad examination of the content and skills in all of the domains. The authors of each volume in this series offer concrete and realistic illustrations and examples, along with reflective exercises. You will find their work to be of exceptional merit, illustrating with insight the depth and interconnectedness of the domains. This series provides the fullest, most contemporary, and most useful information available for the preparation and professional development of principals.

Scott D. Thomson
Executive Secretary
National Policy Board for
Educational Administration

If you would like information about how to become a member of the **School Leadership Library**, please contact

Eye On Education
6 Depot Way West, Suite 106
Larchmont, NY 10538
(914) 883-0551
(914) 833-0761 FAX

ACKNOWLEDGMENTS

Authors wish to thank our spouses Carolyn Hoyle and Gana Crenshaw for support, inspiration, and for editing the manuscript. Our thanks to David Erlandson, a coeditor of the School Leadership Library Series. He is a top scholar in educational administration and a friend. Big thanks also go to assistants Bill Ashworth, Jr., of the Department of Educational Administration, who is a magician with a computer, and Thea Mancini of the Lewisville, Texas, Central Office staff for her dedication and hard work.

Also, we are eternally grateful for the principals, assistant principals, students, faculty, parents, and colleagues who have shared their experiences with us. These personal reflections are the heart of this book.

ABOUT THE AUTHORS

John Hoyle has written or edited several books and has produced 90 articles and book chapters on school organizational and leadership issues. He has served as President of the National Council of Professors of Educational Administration, and Chair of the American Association of School Administrators National Commission on Standards for the Superintendency. Hoyle served as a teacher, coach, and administrator in Midland and Odessa, Texas, and has taught in five universities and in Europe. His latest book is *Leadership and Futuring: Making Visions Happen*, Corwin Press.

Harry Crenshaw holds a Bachelor of Science degree in Chemistry from Southwestern University and a Doctorate in Educational Administration from Texas A&M University. He is a practicing administrator with 16 years experience as a principal. Dr. Crenshaw has also been a visiting professor at Texas A&M and has published numerous articles and one book. He has made several presentations at international, national, and state education conventions.

TABLE OF CONTENTS

PREFACE

Modern schools combine two antagonistic elements. On the one hand they represent the highest in human aspiration for all that is best in life. They have been developed by society to formally prepare children for taking part in the larger society both for their own benefit and for the benefit of society. They promise to give students the skills and understandings that will make them economically productive and socially competent. They also promise to introduce them to realms of beauty and wonder that have enraptured the human soul over the centuries. They aspire to help students be the best that they can be.

But schools, as they have been structured to meet the needs of a large, increasingly diverse population, have become, in too many cases, faceless bureaucracies. People become categorized as "science teachers," "gifted students," "handicapped students," "counselors," "administrators," "minorities," or "parents." Within these categories, the bureaucracy often robs them of their personalities and treats them as interchangeable parts. Job performance and attitudes toward people in other groups are often primarily shaped by the connotations of the group labels that people bear. Because of the specific goals associated with their particular jobs and their stereotyped images of people in other groups, various individuals in the school and its environment often find themselves in unproductive conflict with each other. As long as these individuals are unwilling to search for and accept each other on the basis of their personal value and are unable to perceive what other people in and around the school are feeling and thinking, the activity that takes place in the school is like to be dehumanizing and sterile.

If schools are to function effectively as human organizations to meet human needs, they must be permeated by an atmosphere of interpersonal sensitivity that enables adults and youngsters to genuinely care about each other, look for the best in each other, and seek to help each other. While one could make the case that such an atmosphere ought to occur naturally in an institution dedicated to human growth and development, the sad fact is that too often it does not. Conflicts between teachers and students, teachers and administrators, parents and teachers, parents and students, and administrators and students are so commonplace in schools that they are often accepted as natural. Whether or not they are "natural" is beside the point. They are often unproductive and must be dealt with constructively so that the lofty goals of education may be pursued. An atmosphere of interpersonal productivity must be established and developed.

John Hoyle and Harry Crenshaw take the position that interpersonal sensitivity in the school begins with the principal. If the school climate is to become positive, the principal must personally take the lead in establishing a pattern and model of interpersonal sensitivity. Hoyle and Crenshaw explore the elements of interpersonal sensitivity as they are exhibited by the principal and consider their application with regard to students, teachers, parents, community members, and other persons caught in the stifling web of the school bureaucracy. They recognize that the interpersonal learning that can be fostered in a climate of sensitivity is a type of learning (and reflection of a type of intelligence) that is as valuable as any developed by the school. Hoyle and Crenshaw emphasize the necessity of opening up the lines of communication between people so that they can gain the most from their contact with each other and thereby enhance their combined effort. They present a strong case for demonstrating sensitivity and active support for all children and all adults, regardless of their position, race, economic status, or family influence.

Throughout this book Hoyle and Crenshaw provide practical activities which principals can use to assess and build their own sensitivity with regard to various types of individuals in and around the school. In their final chapter, they propose a strategy for systematically building one's own sensitivity and conclude their book with a proposed activity for moving the entire school toward a school atmosphere that unites rather than divides people.

This is a very practical book for the professional development of either a current or a prospective principal. Interpersonal sensitivity, though only one of the 21 performance domains identified by the National Policy Board for Educational Administration, is a highly critical one. More than one principal, highly skilled in every other area of performance, has failed because of a deficiency in this crucial interpersonal domain. This book can help the principal build both his or her own skill of interpersonal sensitivity and establish an atmosphere of sensitivity that pervades the school.

David A. Erlandson
Alfred P. Wilson

1

WHAT IS INTERPERSONAL SENSITIVITY?

Webster's Ninth New Collegiate Dictionary provides two related, but somewhat contrasting, interpersonal dimensions of "sensitivity." One is "the capacity of being easily hurt"; the other is "awareness of needs and emotions of others." Principals encounter both kinds of sensitivity in themselves and others.

"Oh, don't be so sensitive!" A middle school principal heard these words from his superintendent after the principal told her that a parent had verbally attacked him over a cheerleader selection. Why do we take things so personally and let them eat at us for days? A comment or a memo from an unhappy or uninformed parent or superior can rip the center of our conscious and cause us to seriously reconsider our decision to remain in our current roles. Retirement or running away seems to creep into our interpersonal sensitivities and we lose our perspective about being sensitive to others.

However, it is the second alternative definition which provides the primary basis for our focus on interpersonal sensitivity in principals themselves and others. The National Policy Board for Educational Administration (1993) defines sensitivity as

perceiving the needs and concerns of others; dealing tactfully with others; working with others in emotionally stressful situations or in conflict; managing conflict;

1

obtaining feedback; recognizing multicultural differences; and relating to people of varying backgrounds.

How do school principals who are constantly under personal scrutiny by insensitive parents, extremist groups, teachers, central office administrators, and others manage to be sensitive to the problems of others around them? To be sensitive to others and to help them through difficulties and to reach their goals is a valuable attribute for school principals. Howard Gardner of Harvard University believes that individuals who display strong skills in interpersonal sensitivity are revealing one of the seven phases of intelligence he has identified in human beings. He defines interpersonal intelligence as the capacity to understand individuals, and to use such understanding to interact with such individuals. Certainly, outstanding principals exhibit this phase of intelligence.

However, while the focus of this book is on sensitivity to others, the principal cannot neglect his or her own sensitivities. To express interpersonal sensitivity to others, Gardner believes that one should have intrapersonal intelligence as well. Intrapersonal intelligence is a sensitivity to one's own wishes, fears, dreams, and abilities and the capacity to use such self-knowledge effectively to direct one's life. To be sensitive to others, school principals need to be sensitive to themselves and love and respect themselves—warts and all. In the midst of stress-filled days and the rush of keeping family, friends, and staff happy, criticism is bound to happen to principals. It is easy to say FIDO, i.e., forget it and drive on, but it is very difficult to do. When your pride has been punctured by critics who notice your mistakes of commission or omission, it is very difficult to be kind and sensitive to other people. If you, as principal, are to be a keen perceiver of the needs and concerns of others, you must be kind and sensitive to old number one first. If you cannot forgive yourself for the mistakes you invariably make, then your chances for success as a dynamic principal are diminished considerably. To be sensitive to the needs of others is to be sensitive to your own needs first. Poet Max Ehrmann (1927) said it best about self-respect:

Nurture strength of spirit to shield you in sudden misfortune. But do not distress yourself with imaginings. Many fears are born of fatigue and loneliness. Beyond a wholesome discipline, be gentle with yourself.

If you can learn to be gentle with yourself, you can be more sensitive to others.

In the following story a desperate teacher's career was saved by a sensitive principal who looked beyond the policies:

A young, second-year teacher had a 1-year-old child with a chronic illness which caused the teacher to miss school too frequently. Since the husband traveled in his work and no relatives lived close by, the young teacher had a very difficult time balancing the child's illness with her job and family. Rather than the principal telling the teacher to find a full-time babysitter—which she could not afford—she told her that she would become her team teacher when needed. But the principal told her that she needed some training to be a worthy teammate and would meet at the teacher's convenience for the training sessions. After a few days of the principal filling in, the young teacher's child made a remarkable recovery and could return to the nursery. From that point the second-year teacher became the hardest working and most cooperative teacher in the building. This act of human kindness and sensitivity by the principal was an excellent example of the dynamic and interactive nature of sensitivity.

School principals are often viewed as inflexible rule enforcers who rarely empower teachers and staff to help make decisions that affect them. How long will faculty tolerate and forgive a principal who ignores faculty input on issues about curriculum and instruction? Will creative uses of curriculum materials and novel teaching occur in spite of a principal who refuses to involve others? Obviously a lot of excellent teaching and learning goes on in classrooms by teachers who have learned to by-pass insensitive principals. To avoid conflict with the principal, teachers will usually seek the status quo and teach the same old things in the same old ways and find little joy in the process. All too often teachers working for a "control freak" will do their own thing and not "rock the boat" or attempt anything new for fear of a reprimand from the "boss" down the hall. When this control mindset becomes pervasive among the teaching staff, very little creative sharing of ideas occurs. This form of insensitivity by the building principal is copied by the assistant principals and others with a title or position of authority. Unless teachers, staff, and students sense that the principal cares about them and their needs and concerns and makes a special effort to involve them in the issues that affect them, very little progress will be made toward an empowered, caring community.

According to Carl Glickman (1990), a school staff who works together improves together and feels good about their collective effort. He asserts that, "The more the school works collectively, the more individual differences and tensions between the staff become apparent. These differences will occur because everyone will have a say in decisions and be allowed to express their opinions" (p. 69). Sensitive principals can develop the skills to create schools that inspire those in them to greater accomplishment and satisfaction. Nan Restine (1995) is convinced that ". . . in order to provide meaningful opportunities for learners, meaningful growth opportunities must be provided for those who serve as stewards of student learning" (p. xii). These opportunities for growth include a voice in the ways in which they do their teaching and learning business and the opportunities they have to "sharpen their professional saws." Teachers trapped in an environment of low trust and suspicion resort to cliquish and immature behavior toward colleagues and students. We are strange creatures when our backs are against the walls of paranoia and fear. We strike out at others who are usually innocent victims of our damaged feelings and pride. Caring and sharing power and information does wonders for us. We then do wonders for others under our care.

Most principals believe that they are sensitive in their daily encounters with teachers, staff, parents, community members, and students. However, interpersonal sensitivity is often in the eye of the beholder, which makes the concept that much more difficult to measure or carry out successfully in a complex school setting. In a time of heightened stress on multiculturalism, gender sensitivity, political correctness, and diversity, all principals need to interact and mix with the entire school community more than ever before. When we recognize the need to acknowledge the strength found in difference, we can then empower others to help carry the load of educating each student. The poet Homer said, "Strength is found in feeble arms combined." Bolman and Deal (1993, p. 60) suggest three steps that principals can take to become more sensitive and to empower others in the school community:

1. Open up communications. (Spend time with people. Listen to them. Attend to their feelings, concerns, and aspirations.)

2. Ask for feedback. (Without feedback, leaders easily become blind to how they're really seen. If the feedback is surprising or negative, listen, acknowledge its importance, and share your own feelings.)

3. Empower everyone: (Increase participation, provide support, share information, and move decision making as far down the organization as possible).

SEVEN KEYS TO INTERPERSONAL SENSITIVITY

According to Muse, et al. (1993), principals need to heighten their progress towards greater interpersonal sensitivity. By being aware of the seven key elements within the definition of interpersonal sensitivity (see page 1), principals may be able to prevent staff morale and performance problems before they grow out of proportion or, in the words of deputy Barney Fife, "Nip it in the bud!" The seven key elements listed below are included to help principals be more sensitive.

After completing this book, principals should be aware of skills which will enable them to:

♦ Perceive the needs and concerns of others;
♦ Deal tactfully with others;
♦ Work with others in emotionally stressful situations or conflict;

- Manage conflict;
- Obtain feedback;
- Recognize multicultural differences; and
- Relate to people of different backgrounds.

Each of the seven elements of interpersonal sensitivity is discussed briefly below and alluded to throughout the book. It is important to remember that these elements are benchmarks that keep us reaching for perfection but are rarely achieved. Poet Robert Browning knew about the difficulties of reaching perfection and overcoming human frailties when he wrote, "Man's reach shall exceed his grasp, or what's a heaven for." Our natural human reaction to pressures caused by the mistakes of others or ourselves is to strike back with blame and negativism toward others or ourselves. We want to be sensitive, patient, and tolerant during stressful, disruptive times, but our primitive urges override our best intentions and drag us into insensitive ways of acting. How many times can a school principal be a reactive, insensitive person and maintain the respect required for the position? People are very forgiving up to a point. Asking for forgiveness may work a few times, but eventually others around you will try to avoid you and seek the shadows from your insensitive behaviors and deeds. By attending to these seven elements, principals may avoid many of the pitfalls of insensitivity.

ELEMENT 1: PERCEIVE THE NEEDS AND CONCERNS OF OTHERS

A cold uncaring person can become a warm, caring person by seeking to identify the needs and concerns of others. Human behavior can change—according to learning psychologists and grandparents. As a grandparent, John Hoyle is a much better counselor, storyteller, and fishing buddy than he was as a father. He has more patience, more understanding, and he rarely yells at his grandchildren. If he could redo his dadhood, he would perceive their needs and concerns and be a better dad to his son and daughter. They are remarkable young adults in spite of being reared by an amateur dad. Their greatness came from a remarkable mom. The point is: behavior can and does change.

Education depends on it! You as a school principal can learn the skills to identify the needs and concerns of others and promote a winning interpersonal relations climate in your school. This will help you become a servant leader with a "cause beyond yourself." If you want to be viewed by others as a positive, sensitive, promoter of the welfare of others, then the battle is half won. At least you are aware that you sometimes or often make a mess of things because of your quick trigger which causes pain and discomfort for others—sometimes those you love the most, your family and friends. One way to gain better perception of the needs and concerns of others is by careful observation. Use observation skills effectively to gain information about the needs of others. Observe the behaviors of others and be slow to judge until you "have walked a mile in their shoes." It is amazing how much we can learn about others by merely watching how they interact with those around them. People tend to act in predictable ways. We are creatures of habit, even though our basic personalities are set at conception. A sensitive principal who perfects his or her observation skills can anticipate how people will react to certain situations. This sensitivity can help head off some ill feelings and misunderstandings among teachers, staff, parents, and central office administrators. When a potential conflict situation arises, an aware, sensitive leader can predict the process that will occur between personalities.

Careful reflection and the mental role playing of your mind tapes will prepare you to handle verbal attacks and irrational behavior by angry people. A young school administrator failed to play his mental tapes and could have ended his career in the school business. One evening he received a call from an irate dad who threatened to come to school and "whip his ass" because the principal had disciplined his son for fighting. Without thinking, the young principal's warrior instincts took over and he told the father to "come on down and meet me at the bicycle racks near the school." The principal waited for about 30 minutes and the angry dad never showed. By this time the principal had cooled off and began to feel stupid about what he said to that dad. The father never mentioned the problem again, and the young principal was relieved! He should have been a cool listener and allowed the dad to expel his anger before he opened his big mouth. If the father had met him at those bicycle racks, several things could have happened—not one good for either of them.

The ability to listen carefully and respectfully and keep cool while under verbal attack is a key leadership skill. In most cases irate people, once they have "vented their spleens," will become rational and willing to cooperate with you to find a solution to their problem. A keen, sensitive observer of social interaction has an advantage in stressful school situations. If you can predict with good accuracy what people will say and do in most social interactions, you can assist people through their human frailties and emotional reactions and guide them to work together to create learning communities that respect different people with different ideas and dreams.

By holding our judgment and waiting for the good to appear in people, we avoid a host of problems that can be very difficult to deal with later on. Humorist Will Rogers must have watched people for a long time when he said, "I never met a man I didn't like." Careful observation of the needs, behaviors, and idiosyncrasies of others may not make us like every person on the staff or in the community, but observation and reflection can assist us in increasing our interpersonal sensitivity and concerns for others to help assure that good teaching and mentoring goes on in each classroom.

ELEMENT 2: DEAL TACTFULLY WITH OTHERS

Insensitive principals are often guilty of lack of tact and may not even be aware of it. When teachers and other staff members need to be corrected or assisted with a problem, they do not want the entire world to know about it. Rather than single them out in a gathering or write a memo of reprimand or criticism, call them in to your office or go to a private place and talk personally with them about the issue which concerns you. In most instances, this open communication between the two of you will solve the problem and help avoid unnecessary public or individual embarrassment, anger, or further misinformation.

Choose your spot to lead others to higher achievement and morale. Unless there is a life-threatening, or dangerous situation, rarely call a person to task or attempt to lecture someone in the wrong setting. People must have their dignity respected by their boss, even when the boss thinks the subordinate is way out of line.

Another good practice is to rarely tell jokes or stories about one of the staff unless you are positive that the individual will not be offended. A funny story at the expense of another is never good practice and reveals a lack of tact. Making remarks about a teacher's appearance can be a sensitive area as well. Remarks about a person's clothes can be misconstrued as sexist or too personal and may be considered a form of sexual harassment or poor judgment. Using tact is a sign that you as principal value the dignity and personal feelings of those around you. Work on dealing tactfully with others.

ELEMENT 3: WORK WITH OTHERS IN EMOTIONALLY STRESSFUL SITUATIONS OR CONFLICT

Emotional stress and conflict are always present and are a way of life in school settings. Stress, squabbles, and hurt feelings are all part of human inter-action, and to ignore these problems between teachers, staff, and students is naiveté at its height. Stress and conflict between people are going to occur and the key to interpersonal sensitivity by the principal is recognizing them and dealing with them in a prompt and professional manner. Allowing two teachers to continue an ongoing verbal war of words and ignoring the animosity of one person toward another are tantamount to professional negligence and cowardice.

Stress and conflict can only be managed—they will never be stopped—by recognizing them, clarifying them, and bringing the people together to talk through their differences. Stress and conflict ignored or hidden ruins marriages and friend-ships and can definitely ruin the morale in a school. A proper balance of stress and conflict and progress go together in productive learning organizations because strong willed and creative people are usually risk-takers who plow ahead. These strong personalities can offend others without realizing it and without a sensitive facilitator, stress and conflict can create hard feelings and block open communication.

The old cliché, "name it to tame it," certainly applies to stress and conflict management. Recognize emotional stress and conflict for the natural behaviors they are and take steps to clarify them, reduce them, and keep spirited people working together for the welfare of kids. Emotional stress and related conflict can literally cripple the morale of everyone in a school setting. You, as principal, must be vigilant in looking for signs of emotional "burnout," anger, and other morale busters that diminish individual and school productivity. Work with your site-based team to identify signs of stress and conflict and plan workshops on stress management and conflict resolution.

ELEMENT 4: MANAGE CONFLICT

Rudyard Kipling wrote: "If you can keep your head when all about you are losing theirs and blaming it on you. . . ." The principal who reads this introductory line to Kipling's poem can resonate with the feeling expressed. Conflict among people in groups and organizations is pervasive and inevitable, and the principal usually becomes the lightning rod for much of the interpersonal conflict that exists in the school. There is conflict among students, between teachers and students, among teachers, between teachers and parents, and between students and their parents.

Whenever people are engaged in an activity that occupies a major portion of their time and attention, they have strong (though not always clear) expectations for it. Schools stir up strong and often antagonistic feelings in their various stakeholders. This results in conflict, and it is a central part of the principal's job to manage that conflict. Note that we had said "manage" and not "eliminate" the conflict. As we have noted, interpersonal conflict will occur in the school and its immediate environment. The challenge to the principal is to use the diverse expectations of individuals and groups to shape a situation that is responsive to their individual needs and their common purpose.

The sensitive principal takes the time to learn and appreciate how students, faculty members, parents, and others in the school context see the world around them and what they expect from their participation in the school. This understanding enables the principal to perceive where fundamental agreements between antagonists exist and where their expectations are negotiable. It also shows the principal where expectations need to be raised. Most teachers and parents want what is best for students. Most students generally want to succeed in school. The sensitive principal can capitalize on these positive desires to move through conflict and enable everyone to win.

ELEMENT 5: OBTAIN FEEDBACK

Solicit the perceptions and concerns of others, and seek information from others. Thank God for school custodians who love kids and who have big ears. Inside trader information didn't begin on Wall Street; it started between school principals and custodians. After-school fights between students, concealed weapons in lockers, problems between teachers and parents, and kids smoking in the hallway, are part of a good custodian's information base. A smart school principal considers that custodian a member of the management team.

A sensitive school principal is often a veritable gad-a-bout who constantly talks with kids, teachers, parents, community members, police officers, ministers, and his/her staff. Talking to kids can help a principal solve some complex problems. A principal in Texas found out about the power of information from the mouths of students. During a lunch period a 7th grade boy who worked in the cafeteria for his meal said he needed to talk with the principal. The principal really liked this kid and had tried to help him by giving him the lunchroom job and having friendly chats with him daily. He was a poor kid who literally lived on the other side of the tracks and was rarely seen with any friends. This adult-kid friendship between the boy and the principal led to a breakthrough in a series of teenage gang crimes.

When the principal asked the boy to tell her what was on his mind, his eyes filled with tears. His story overwhelmed the principal. He told of getting mixed up with a gang of boys who were breaking into homes and stealing electronic equipment, bicycles, and other valuable property and hiding the stolen goods in a vacant house. The principal called the juvenile authorities and told them about the crimes and asked the authorities to go easy on her young friend who had the courage to turn in his buddies. The police were amazed that the principal was able to help them solve a series of crimes that they had been trying to solve for months. Seek information from all who will offer it. You may not solve crimes, but you can become a sensitive, good listener and constant learner.

A sensitive principal is not only a receiver of feedback but is also a sender of feedback. Principals who provide constant feedback and celebrate successes of others have higher morale and winning school climates. Motivation theorists tell us that recognition is not a primary motivator. That is, recognition for personal and professional accomplishments in and of itself is not a prime motivator. However, people who are never or rarely receive feedback and recognition for their achievements become so dissatisfied that they lose their desire to produce at higher levels.

The age of accountability has become so powerful in education that all of us feel "under the gun." School principals often feel that the central office, the school board, the public and the state department are watching every move they make in hope of catching them in a mistake. This seems to be an irony on the education scene today, given the rich background of literature on site-based decision-making, total quality management, and learning communities. What is being written is not being played out in the schools across America. The pressures on school principals created by school boards, state agencies, and radical community groups belie the more human side of leadership which calls for recognition for a job well done and support by parents and community in the education process. The old "walk the walk and talk the talk" phrase rings empty in the halls of many schools where the cries for accountability have drowned out the cheers of recognition for teachers, and especially for school principals. Therefore, where fear and distrust are brought on by extreme pressures of accountability, sensitive principals need to strive for greater amounts of feedback, praise, and recognition for the efforts of the teaching and other staff members.

Turn faculty meetings into pep rallies for staff victories, victories for student achievements, teacher creativity, birthdays, recognition for "random acts of kindness," and other awards to celebrate the greatness shown daily by members of the school staff. It is sad indeed to hear an educator tell another that the educator has never received feedback from the principal, let alone be congratulated by the principal on anything. Interpersonal sensitivity starts with you the principal; catch staff and students in the act of succeeding and provide feedback to them and others. By receiving and giving positive feedback, the morale and the performance will constantly improve.

ELEMENT 6: RECOGNIZE MULTICULTURAL DIFFERENCES

Diversity and multiculturalism is a reality in America and particularly in our schools. By the year 2000, in most major cities and in some states, the minority population will be in the majority and the number of minority students will continue to grow. These demographic changes have heightened the interests in the ethnic and cultural roots of all Americans. Even though many people and principals celebrate America's diversity, many people do not. As a result, equality has failed to exist in communities and schools throughout our land. Attempts to develop multicultural education programs in our schools have a mixed record of success. Much has been written about the purpose of multicultural education, but not enough has been done to assure its success.

To be effective, multicultural education must be integrated into the educational environment in school programs and not merely by an add-on. To guide this integration, principals must first be sensitive to the uniqueness of each person in their schools and develop a richer knowledge base and a set of attitudes and values that will assure the inclusion of multicultural programming. Principals have not always been prepared to understand the motives, profiles, and perceptions of today's multicultural, multilingual, and multiethnic school populations (Baptise, 1988).

To become an outstanding principal, you must continue learning about the differences among the people in your community and the students you serve. This knowledge helps you use the strengths and beauty of those differences to unite the school into a learning community which respects the unique gifts that each student, teacher, and parent brings to the school.

To recognize multicultural differences is one thing, but to do something about it is another. You need to develop servant leadership behaviors and attempt to reach for a "cause beyond oneself" in thought and deed for all children and youth and adults.

Johnathan Kozol (1995) observed this kind of sensitivity and leadership embodied in Manuel Rodriguez, principal of P.S. 65 in New York City's South Bronx. His students, among the poorest and most neglected in America, live with poverty, violence, disease, and life-consuming fires in dilapidated tenant housing. Rodriguez told Kozol (p. 64):

> Some of our children have been horribly disfigured in these fires. I notice, though, that the other children treat them kindly and do not make fun of them. There is a protective feeling that can be extraordinarily moving. There is nothing predatory in these children. They know that the world does not much like them and they try hard to be good to one another. No matter how disfigured they may be, I find these children beautiful.

This deep and abiding sensitivity for these scarred ghetto children is an example of how an inner city principal can be sensitive to multicultural differences through his love and compassion. People in your school and community need a principal who has sensitivity, compassion, and respect for them. They need a principal who will observe, listen, and learn about their daily struggles, cultures, and human needs. They need a principal who makes every effort to "walk in their shoes" and look into their hearts and eyes for their humanness.

ELEMENT 7: RELATE TO PEOPLE OF DIFFERENT BACKGROUNDS

This element of interpersonal sensitivity is tied closely with Element 5. Relating in personal and meaningful ways with people from different cultures and backgrounds is not a simple matter of shallow conversation and traditional ways of doing things.

Imagine this: You have been hired as principal of a high school, middle school, or elementary school with a student population of 26% black, 24% Hispanic, 30% Anglo, 15% Vietnamese, and 5% Native American. About half of your students are from single-parent homes. Half are from middle-class backgrounds, and the remaining 50% are from working class or poor families. More than 40% of the students are on free or reduced-cost lunches. Also, 9% of your students are exceptionally gifted. Your teaching staff is 75% Anglo, 15% black, and 14% Hispanic. Among your younger teachers only 3% are minority because your school district has been unable to attract qualified minority candidates to teach in your school.

How will you be sensitive to the needs of these people with such diverse backgrounds? What kinds of curricula, teaching strategies, and community partnerships will you promote to attain equity and a positive climate for your school family? What can you do to increase your knowledge and sensitivity of different learning styles and teaching styles to help each student and teacher succeed? Will you, in the words of James Banks (1989, pp. 19–20), "transform the school so that male and female students, exceptional students, as well as students from diverse cultural, social class, racial and ethnic groups, will experience an equal opportunity to learn in school." It is impossible to see the world through the eyes of people who are different from us racially and culturally. However, it is possible to develop a knowledge about their backgrounds and to continue to sensitize your actions and words to reflect respect for each person in your school community. Suggestions on ways to help you and your school family became more sensitive to the diverse cultures and backgrounds of others are found in Chapter 2.

The rest of this book follows up on the ideas presented thus far. We hope that you, the busy reader, will find value in each of the chapters. Unless principals strive to become more sensitive to the needs of others and to strengthen their individual moral centers, schools will never become the kinds of places where children learn tolerance and self respect. Chapter 2 focuses on the need for principals to help create a caring school for all students. How to create a family atmosphere and a supportive learning community is emphasized. Actual cases and stories are highlighted. Chapter 3 presents the need for principal sensitivity to faculty and staff with suggestions to help principals develop greater sensitivity. Cases and stories reinforce the direction of the chapter. Chapter 4 provides a rationale for sensitivity towards parents and the community and presents suggestions to help principals improve their skills and knowledge base. Real-world cases are included as examples of how principals have successfully used interpersonal sensitivity with parents and others in the community. The chapter centers on ways to make the entire community sensitive to the needs of each student. Actual cases are included. Chapter 5 helps principals cope with the problem of being caught between the demands of the central office and the building staff. If each school is to have reasonable autonomy from the central office, how does a principal remain sensitive to individuals who carry out district policies and operations while continuing to free his or her staff to create curriculum and teaching strategies unique to the school? Chapter 6 helps principals develop strategies for building sensitivity, both personally and organizationally A skill building activity is included with each chapter to help you build your skills in interpersonal sensitivity. Good luck!

SKILL BUILDING ACTIVITIES

1. List three of the most recent occasions where you seriously tried to perceive the needs and concerns of a person/s in the following group:
    a. student
    b. teacher
    c. staff member
    d. parent
    e. central office person
2. Describe an event where you displayed
    a. Poor tact toward another person.
    b. Good tact toward another person.
3. a. Recall an event where a teacher showed signs of high emotional stress. What did you do?
    b. How have you tried to manage conflict between members of your staff? Give an example.

4. Describe one or more instances of interpersonal conflict in your school that you were expected to mediate.
   a. Did you fully understand how each of the individuals or groups in the conflict saw the situation?
   b. Did you understand what each of the individuals or groups in the conflict expected from their involvement in the school?
   c. Were you able to work with the conflicting parties to shape an agreement that served their needs as well as those of the entire school? If so, how were you able to do this? If not, why not?
5. a. What processes do you use to obtain feedback from others?
   b. What techniques do you use to provide feedback to others?
6. a. List two recent activities or workshops you helped plan on multicultural differences and multicultural education.
   b. What are two knowledge areas where you need more information to help you become more sensitive?
7. Think of a time when you felt a little awkward in conversing and relating to a person or person with backgrounds different from your own. How did you feel? What did you learn?

2

BEING SENSITIVE TO STUDENTS

How sensitive can we be with students? A seventh grade science teacher learned a lesson about student sensitivity when he befriended a boy named Danny. Danny was a 16-year-old, 230-pound, mackinaw-wearing, slow learner who was mainstreamed into his class. He was dirty, he carried the odors of campfires, bacon fat, and sweat along with a permanent backpack which held an assortment of rocks, dried worms, and live frogs. Danny was one of eight in what is now called a dysfunctional family, and his vision was on the next meal and the last class bell which would free him to roam the woods in search of live or dead critters.

The teacher liked Danny from the start. He tried to be sensitive to his world and adjusted his teaching to accommodate his intelligence. While other students were learning the structure of the atom, Danny was constructing papier-mâché volcanoes and dinosaurs in back of the room. When Danny finished a volcano masterpiece, the teacher would call him to the front of the class and ask him to demonstrate his volcanic eruption with a mixture of baking soda and vinegar. He would laugh, pick up the pieces and return to the back of the class to begin another work of art. His classmates were warned to never laugh at him or they would answer to the teacher.

After several dinosaur and volcano demonstrations and the teacher's effusive words of praise each time, Danny grew to respect and love his favorite teacher. He began bringing him gifts from his night hunts in the woods. Bugs, bats, and spiders were usual offerings which the teacher placed in jars on the shelf for Danny's classmates to see.

Danny and this teacher were tight, while his other teachers dreaded each class he attended. Danny merely went about his own business and didn't talk much with his classmates. One winter morning, Danny walked in carrying a big paper sack which was moving. Danny asked, "Teacher, do you want a snake?" The teacher asked, "What kind?" He retorted, "A live 'en." Before the teacher could say anything, Danny reached in his sack and extracted a three-foot long live snake. Trying to hide his stark terror, the teacher led Danny and his snake to the lab closet and found a big jar in which Danny placed his agitated serpent. The teacher later pickled the critter and placed a big label on the jar which read "Danny's Snake."

One classmate named Macky was the brightest and the most mischievous student in the class. He would pinch and poke others, talk back to the teacher and others, and was a constant nuisance. The teacher warned him several times about his behavior and had threatened to take him to see the principal and his paddle. One morning in science lab, Macky decided to yank a girl's hair. The teacher said, "That's it, Macky, come with me to the office." About that time the teacher heard someone running to his aid. It was Danny who picked Macky up (desk and all), slammed him against the wall, and asked, "You want me to whup him for you, teacher?" The teacher calmly asked Danny to put Macky down and told him that he would handle it. Danny would have totally eliminated Macky if the teacher hadn't stopped him.

That teacher has reflected on that incident many times and realized that he had created a loyal and somewhat lethal friend in Danny. Two years after that incident the teacher was an assistant principal in a nearby town and returned to visit a friend at his old school. As he was parking his car he saw, coming the wrong way on a one-way street, an old Ford with smoke pouring from its exhaust and the ham of an arm hanging over the driver side door. The car stopped in the middle of the street, the door flew open, and out ran Danny to grab his former teacher and pick him up and greet him with a big hug. He told the teacher that he had quit school and had a job in a salvage yard, and he beamed with pride as he pointed to his smoking old Ford. Danny was, in his own eyes, a rich man. Was his teacher too sensitive to Danny? You be the judge.

But that experience with Danny was several years ago. Are kids different today? Julia Stratton (1995) believes they are. Social change and mixed signals about the values underlying the path to success in business and government leave today's children and youth wondering about their future roles in American life. Stratton writes that,

> Today's students seem different because they are different. Their world is far removed from what ours was in decades past and has affected them in both positive and negative ways. . . . As "Generation X" grows up witnessing the videotaped Rodney King beating and subsequent Los Angeles riots, Clarence Thomas-Anita Hill hearings, abortion clinic killings, the O.J. case, and the bombing of the Alfred P. Murrah Building in Oklahoma City, some would argue that young people have lost not only their boundaries of right and wrong, but also their hope and faith in a better tomorrow (pp. iii & 7).

The latest statistics confirm the reasons that children and youth worry about their future:

- In 1993, we had more than 14.6 million children living in poverty, including 22.7% of children under 18, and nearly three times that of our international competitors, according to the Economic Policy Institute.
- 78% of students have cheated.
- 29% have considered suicide.
- 35% of students surveyed said they would engage in sex without a condom.
- The number of teenagers and young adults with AIDS increased by more than 75% between 1990 and 1992, and AIDS is now the sixth leading cause of death among youth ages 13–24.

♦   From 1986 to 1991 the number of youths and teenagers killed by firearms rose 59%, from 3,373 to 5,356 annually, according to the FBI (Stratton, 1995).

Some principals realize that today's kids face a troubled world, truly love kids, and try to fill each day talking to and encouraging them to excel, to become leaders, to help others, to respect their teachers, parents, and their classmates. Some principals look for students who look lost, lonely, or confused and help them solve their problems. Principals who express this profound sensitivity for students are models for others who desire to have the same capacity for caring and helping each student who needs them.

Some principals are reluctant to express compassion for any student for fear of losing their image of toughness as the top authority figure in the school. A principal was overheard telling a first-year teacher, "Do not smile at your students until Christmas and then only between classes." "And remember," he continued, "You are their teacher, not their friend." How sad that this is the message that often prevails in the classrooms and schools across America.

We are reluctant to express sensitivity to students because we fear that they may forget "their place" in the school community hierarchy. "If you give 'em an inch, they'll take a mile," is the logo in many teachers' lounges and principals' staff meetings. This mindset has been around since the one room school and the *McGuffey Reader*. However, increased incidents of student violence against teachers and administrators have driven school leaders to install "zero tolerance" and other behavior controls, including police in the halls and on school grounds. How do school principals balance the need to keep the lid on trouble makers, disruption, and school violence while being sensitive to the needs of the majority of the students who need quality leadership and compassion?

SCENARIO #1: A STUDENT NAMED JACK

Jack is an average student in middle school. Jack makes average grades and is seldom in trouble, but occasionally he is "all boy." Jack's parents both work and are supportive of the school. They keep in touch with Jack's teachers and always support the school when Jack needs to be disciplined.

One day, Jack is jovially walking down the hall and asks to see you, the principal, when you have time. You have phone calls to return and have several meetings with teachers. You know Jack and don't perceive that he was asking for help for a serious problem. In a joking manner, you respond to Jack by saying you will see him later.

This is a good example of a lack of sensitivity between a principal and a student. What message was conveyed to the student? First, you said, "I'm too busy and I don't think your problem is very serious." This may, in fact, have been the case, but Jack's perception may be that he doesn't matter and you don't care. Second, it places you, the principal, in a precarious situation if a real problem emerges before you respond to the child. How do you defend a lost opportunity?

Some damage control could have been implemented by you if Jack was called to the office in a timely manner. At that time, you could show concern for Jack and listen to his problem or need. Acknowledge his feelings and try to restate what you have just heard from Jack. Proceed, based on the stated problem and your experience.

A better response would have been to ask Jack, in a caring manner, if he could summarize his problem. After hearing the problem, you may have decided to immediately deal with Jack or explained that you are interested in helping, but that several others have problems and that you will call him later when you can talk longer. You should then have asked him if that's OK with him. In doing this, you would have shown concern yet maintained the flexibility to control your time.

In *Amazing Grace*, Jonathan Kozol (1995) tells about the frustrations of trying to appeal to an insensitive Congress and other policymakers to make education an equal opportunity plan for all children. He writes about how the conditions of poverty and the decay of inner cities have left a dark hole in the soul of America. He senses a world that will grow more hostile and divided unless the children of America are treated with compassion and the chance to grow up in better-funded and community-centered schools. Kozol has turned to inner city church leaders who are sensitive and willing to take action to reverse the growing decay of the moral center of urban America.

THE NEED FOR COMPREHENSIVE SERVICES FOR ALL STUDENTS

Much has been written and disseminated about the total service school or the integration of education and human services. Many articles have been written, and projects stressing collaborative services have begun throughout America. This recent movement toward comprehensive services is reminiscent of the antipoverty programs of the Johnson Presidency in the 1960's. This effort to bring social, health, and government agencies in to assist school personnel to educate and support the well-being of our children is a good idea and is helping underfunded and harried teachers, counselors, and administrators do their jobs. However, most schools do not yet have an integrated support system to help with problems created by poverty, family violence, and inadequate healthcare services. School principals are faced with the challenge of seeking these services from civic groups, businesses, or individuals who are willing to give time and money to school needs.

Each day in America more children are abused, go hungry, and turn to drugs. A recent report by the Carnegie Council on Adolescent Development reported that 19 million children between the ages of 10–14 are neglected and that many of them will become casualties of AIDS, violence, poverty, and poor education unless our national leaders act soon. The report reveals that this age group suffers more assaults than any other age group, are having sex more, and are being murdered more. Two-thirds have tried alcohol, and a third have tried illicit drugs. Among the other findings in the report are:

+ One in five adolescents is growing up in poverty.
+ Half of all children will live with only one parent at some point in their lives.

- Parent involvement in education declines by the time students reach middle school and high school.

- The birth rate among adolescent girls is growing fastest in the under-15 age group.

- Twenty-seven percent of eighth graders spent 2 or more hours at home alone after school, increasing their chances of being involved in drugs, crime, or sexual activity.

- In the past 2 years, academic achievement levels of eighth graders have remained virtually stagnant; as adults many will not be able to keep up with a technology-based global economy.

A solution to these problems is not simple, but the report calls for organizing school systems into smaller, more intimate places to learn and train teachers and principals to deal with adolescents and develop stronger links between education and health. Also, community centers are needed for gathering places after school and at other times when students have no supervision at home (Woestendiek, October 12, 1995, p. 7A, *Houston Chronicle*).

Effective school research and all school reform efforts call for extensive involvement of parents and school patrons in school affairs. Schools which include parental and community member input into site-based teams and other activities are more likely to have fewer student behavior problems, better attendance, more instructional resources, higher teacher morale and higher student achievement. Schools and principals who merely play at the game of parent and community involvement are less effective in serving the needs of the students and the community. Joining hands to strengthen the safety net for all children in the community is the primary need for all schools, and school principals must take the lead in constructing the net.

Changes in family structures and lifestyles which include working moms and greater numbers of single parents have pushed the school to assume more of the traditional parental functions and responsibilities. Therefore it is imperative that schools encourage the integrated service concept. David Elkind (1995, September) reflects on the major transformation that schools have undergone in postmodern times of the 1990s by writing, ". . . Our schools today are providing much more in the way of child care, education for children with special needs, child support services, sex education, drug education, and parent education than they did in the modern era" (p. 14). Principals need to tell this story to all who will listen and ask for help in building lives and communities through the total service school. Legislators and education agency administrators must realize the changing nature of schooling and the need for greater funding and support if schools are to be truly reformed.

Research efforts to explore the benefits of total service or integrated service schools have given few clear answers as to their effectiveness. The programs are varied and communities differ, which makes for difficult research design. However, extensive research efforts must be made to guide the direction of school reform. According to Michael Knapp (1995, May), it is vital to continue the search for clues to improving integrated service schools. He believes that, ". . . There is a sufficient number and variety of investments in comprehensive, collaborative service initiatives to afford numerous opportunities for learning and various forms of 'natural experiments.' And the children and families who are recipients of integrated services are too needy and too numerous to ignore" (p.15). A new Center for the Study and Implementation of Collaborative Learning Communities is underway at Texas A&M University. The center housed in the College of Education will study ways to combine the services of education, health, social welfare, juvenile justice and families to make them more cost effective and beneficial for children and youth and their families. Natural experiments by center staff and practitioners will provide valuable insights into ways in which all human service agencies can work together to heal and educate a society that grows more complex each year.

CHAMPIONS FOR CHILDREN

A report by the American Association of School Administrators, *Champions for Children* (1979), called for administrators to become strong advocates for children and youth. The writers defined that role as ". . . advocates for children and youth as human beings, as citizens, and as learners." The need for this report and its plea is so great in the 1990's because the plight of children and youth has worsened since 1979. The report included warning signs that we failed to heed (pp. vi, vii):

- ◆ The dramatically changing family structure in our society;
- ◆ The retreat from integrated education and from affirmative action which have been the paths toward a goal of "one nation undivided";
- ◆ The "taxpayer revolt" which has fallen unevenly upon public education and, thus, on our children and youth;
- ◆ The grossly disproportionate share of unemployment borne by our urban, predominately minority, youth; and
- ◆ The Juvenile Justice System which causes "status offenders" to languish in jail while felonious youth are freed.

Today we could add to that warning list the increased attacks on school curriculum by groups who have a narrow agenda for the education of children and youth. The time has come for school principals to step up and champion the cause of children and youth. This bold action will help change the image of the school principal from a budget manager and building custodian to a visionary for the welfare of all in his or her school community. This sensitivity for the welfare of children and youth is the best solution for turning schools into exciting learning communities. The following tips from *Champions for Children* will help you become a better champion for children (p. 21):

- ◆ Strive to know better the children and youth of your community, their backgrounds, culture and values.
- ◆ Seek to overcome "childhood amnesia," the inability to recall your own view of the world from a child's perspective.
- ◆ Treat children and youth as human beings, as people.

+ Provide them with every possible opportunity to develop their individuality, and uniqueness and to find dignity in who and what they are.

+ Treat them as citizens. Don't join those who clamor for law and order for themselves but seek to deny it to children and youth; hypocrisy only widens the generation gap.

+ Zealously guard their freedoms because in doing so you guard your own.

+ Seek not everything they want, but seek for them everything they need.

+ Hold them accountable for fulfilling their responsibilities, especially their responsibilities as citizens and learners.

+ Help them develop the skills to cope with their environment and the skills to improve that environment when necessary.

+ Expect a lot of them and you'll get it; don't and you won't.

Being a champion for children is not easy when some teachers, parents, and central office administrators are attempting to dictate how you spend your time. Paperwork and report writing are relentless, and the phone just keeps on ringing. You just can't find the time to champion the kids. However, life as a school principal can be pretty miserable if the kids are not part of your daily contacts. One of the authors witnessed a heart warming example of a principal who is truly a champion for kids. The principal of a career center in west Texas took him on a tour of his beautiful new facility. Included in the tour were classroom visits. One class was presenting team speech projects which centered on the language—spoken and nonverbal—in Charley Brown cartoons. One small Hispanic boy named Jesus was playing the role of Snoopy and his only line was a resounding "Woof!" He said it well and with confidence. Tears welled up in the eyes of the principal who whispered, "I am so proud of Jesus, whom I have known for 5 months. He is extremely shy, and to my knowledge has never spoken in public before." A small breakthrough, but for that caring, sensitive principal it made his day. He modeled what is called "a cause beyond oneself."

MULTICULTURAL SENSITIVITY FOR KIDS

Multicultural sensitivity starts with you the principal. Students with different cultural roots and linguistic skills must be prized as gifts to each school. Multicultural education needs to be integrated throughout the school curriculum and in the "feel" of the school. This open and sensitive approach is the only way that each and every child will feel loved and respected as a human being. Lyn Miller-Lachman and Lorraine S. Taylor have written an excellent book that should be read by all educators looking for ideas on improving multicultural sensitivity. They believe that too many educators are culturally insensitive and assert that much more emphasis needs to be placed on preservice and inservice education of teachers and administrators in the areas of cultural diversity and multiethnic literature. Educators need to be made aware of the changing cultural patterns in most school communities. Major groups, i.e., African-American, Latino, Asian-American and American Indian are obviously different from each other, and many differences exist within each major group. Lachman and Taylor (1995, p. 26) observe that, ". . . Many school districts have developed successful, comprehensive programs in which student achievement has improved, intergroup relations are more positive, and community and family involvement have increased. As diverse cultural and linguistic groups have become more involved in their positive identity and preservation of their cultures and languages, the names of these groups have become an important aspect of empowerment." This respect and recognition of cultures different from one's own is the first step toward empowering others to also respect difference and to realize the strength found in "feeble arms combined."

CULTIVATING THE CULTURE

In farming, the land must first be cultivated to encourage the seed to sprout. A school principal must also cultivate the school setting to encourage love and respect to sprout and grow to maturity. If this step is not taken, a field of different languages, dress, foods, music, folkways, ancestors, stories about heroes and heroines may never blossom. Nurturing the rich base of multiculturalism will help reduce the weeds of bigotry, bias, and boredom, and eliminate most of the pests of resentment, restriction, and ridicule. This open awareness and cultivation of difference is a primary reason that some schools outperform others and disciplinary problems and vandalism are minimal. This declaration of respect for difference has a dramatic positive impact on the attitudes and behavior of staff and students, and the walls of prejudice crumble. The walls that divide ethnic and racial groups, academic and career education faculties, teachers and administrators, parents and educators, and students and the community are gradually removed. A multiculturally sensitive school principal with the heart and head for equity and opportunity for all students and faculty can be a "wall buster." The words of Robert Frost, the American poet, might well be applied to schools of the future: ". . . Something there is that doesn't love a wall, that wants it down." How does a sensitive principal go about busting the walls of ignorance and prejudice to produce a school for all students? The following suggestions may help:

♦ Form a "Respect for All" task force. Charge this group to help identify all to the cultures and ethnic groups in the school community. Record the names and addresses of representatives from each group and plan events that emphasize the customs, language, music, heroes, heroines, foods, dances, and history of each group. This task force is responsible with your supervision for arranging these events and for inviting the entire community to participate.

♦ Conduct periodic climate assessments. Several excellent school climate assessment instruments are available to measure opinions of teachers, staff, students, and community about the morale and feelings of success in the school. This climate information may not pinpoint the exact cause of low morale or always give a clear picture of the entire school climate, but the data may point to a growing problem that can be solved before it becomes a serious problem. These climate instruments have proven to be helpful in checking the climate pulse of schools:

- School Profile: Climate—Jim Sweeney, Iowa State University, College of Education, Des Moines, IA 50011

- Learning Climate Inventory—John Hoyle, Climate Research Association, 8409 Whiterose Court, College Station, TX 77845

- Pupil Control Inventory—Wayne Hoy, Department of Educational Administration, 301 Ramseyer Hall The Ohio State University, Columbus, OH 43210-1177

- Student Opinion Inventory—Teacher National Study of School Evaluation, 5201 Leesburg Pike, Falls Church, Va. 22041

- Teacher Opinion Survey—Student National Study of School Evaluation, 5201 Leesburg Pike, Falls Church, VA 22041

- Secondary School Attitude Survey—John Hoyle, Climate Research Associates, 8409 Whiterose Court, College Station, TX 77845

- School Climate Survey (form A)—National Association of Secondary Principals, 1904 Association Drive, Reston, VA 22091

- For other instruments and more information see Hoyle, J., English, F., and Steffy, B. (1994). *Skills for Successful School Leaders*. Chapter Two. Arlington, VA: American Association of School Administrators, 1801 North Moore Street, 22209-9988 (703) 875-0748

SCENARIO #2:
CLIMATE FOR SUCCESS OR FAILURE?

A supportive learning community emphasizing a family atmosphere has been identified as one of the success factors of effective schools. This requires being sensitive to the way students feel and perceive how they are accepted, their comfort zone, and the order in the school.

At Sam Rayburn Middle School in Bryan, Texas, working with the effective schools model, an effort was begun to improve instruction and learning in the school. In order to make changes affecting instruction/learning, the first thing done was to assess what was needed. Using two questionnaires (TASSP Student Opinion Survey and the Secondary School Attitude Inventory), one need identified was that students felt they were not treated with respect.

In addressing this issue, a staff development program was established by the Building Leadership Team (site-based, decision-making body). The emphasis was on how to use various strategies to help students establish and maintain positive perceptions and how to plan for this dimension of learning. An evaluation method was also established.

In being sensitive to students, teachers had to establish a relationship with each student. As a result, students felt accepted by their teachers. To accomplish this, activities were designed to help teachers show their concern for students. One important item was to learn how to listen with respect. Another area was teacher attitudes. Teachers often say they believe all children can learn, but their actions betray them. Techniques for monitoring personal attitudes reflected in teacher behaviors in terms of classroom interactions were explored. Techniques, such as how to respond positively to students' answers, questioning techniques, classroom organization, lesson planning, cooperative learning, teaming, motivation techniques and mediation techniques, were included in this staff development program. Classroom tasks were also stressed, using the idea of "what will I do to help students." If students develop a sense of academic trust, believing they can perform the tasks asked of them, they will perceive that school is a good and comfortable place to be. Activities designed to show teachers how to relate to interests and goals were also included. This involved the use of academic data by both the teacher and student. Teachers were taught to take aggregate test data and grades to analyze the curriculum and disaggregated data to help students develop personal goals.

At the same time that the staff was addressing the relationship between learning and acceptance, they were also concentrating on establishing clear policies regarding the discipline and safety of students. Included in this was educating both the faculty and student body in policies and consequences.

Classroom climate does not just happen by accident. It must be carefully planned and monitored. Therefore, it is imperative that administrators proactively promote activities that demonstrate sensitivity to student needs. This program of staff development was devised and implemented over a 3-year period. The results were evaluated by comparing the results of the climate surveys from each year. Also, a comparison of state-administered test scores was used to evaluate academic progress. Other indicators used were attendance rate, dropout rate, and failure rate.

The focus of all of the staff development was being sensitive to student needs. It took many forms, from planning programs and activities for building students' feelings of acceptance in the school to developing personal attention of teachers for each student. This included improving instruction so students could be more successful. The results were exciting. Test scores rose, failure and dropout rates declined, attendance improved, and the surveys showed greater student satisfaction. As a bonus, for two consecutive years, Rayburn was selected by the public as its favorite school in an area which includes several school districts and over 30 schools.

Sensitivity for students takes two forms: sensitivity for the individual and sensitivity for the group. The above scenarios relate to each in the hope that the reader will perceive that sensitivity can be planned and must be actively developed.

CONCLUSIONS

Being sensitive to students is the only pathway to authentic success in the school principalship. Kids need a "real person" they can admire, who is not out of their reach. A story is told by Norman Irons of a 5-year-old boy who was awakened by a thunder storm, which made him run crying in fear to his daddy's bedside. His dad said, "Don't worry, son, don't be afraid of the storm. God loves you." The frightened little boy quickly responded, "But Daddy, I want love with the skin on it." Children and youth in your school want "love with the skin on it," not some distant power in an office down the hall who is in charge of books, banquets, buses, and budgets. Don't forget that the fifth and most important "b" word is "bolster." Bolster each child with the support he or she needs to gain self-respect and respect for others in the school community.

SKILL BUILDING ACTIVITIES

Table 2.1 provides the Principal's Interpersonal Sensitivity for Students Inventory. Use it in the following activities to assess and build your interpersonal sensitivity to students.

1. Use the inventory form to assess your sensitivity to students in your school.
2. Ask a group of teachers in your school to use the inventory to assess themselves in the same way.
3. Together with these teachers, use the results of the survey to make plans for building a school climate that is sensitive to and accepting of each child in the school.

TABLE 2.1. PRINCIPAL'S INTERPERSONAL SENSITIVITY FOR STUDENTS INVENTORY

(Check the Appropriate Blank.)

	Yes	Sometimes	Rarely
1. I try to recall what it is like to be a child or youth again.			
2. I really listen to students when they talk to me.			
3. I spend time learning about the various ethnic groups.			
4. I model respect and sensitivity for students from all economic and racial groups.			
5. I work with staff to develop integrated curriculum for multicultural education.			
6. I encourage various social, civic, and business groups to help me help my kids.			
7. I ask teachers to gather perceptions from students about how they feel about the school and themselves.			
8. I strive to plan recognition days and programs for the students.			
9. I seek out lonely "isolated" students and try to help them.			

10. I find the time to talk with individual students about their hopes, fears, and dreams.			
11. I strive to create a comprehensive service program for my students.			
12. I treat each student as a citizen with "rights."			
13. I strive to catch and reward students in "acts of success."			
14. I see beauty and hope in each student.			
15. I hold myself and my students responsible for their own successes and failures.			

3

INTERPERSONAL SENSITIVITY WITH FACULTY AND STAFF

Yes, kids are the most important people in your school. And, yes, they are the reason you do what you do. However, the teachers and other staff members make it all happen for the kids. How you treat each teacher and other adults in the school family is usually the way they treat the kids. If you are sensitive to their needs and problems and keep an open mind about ways of doing things that will benefit the students, the behavior will rub off on the staff and benefit the kids. You can still run the school and have an open, caring leaning climate where respect, freedom, and responsibility are intact.

Scott Thomson (1990) recognizes the importance of strong interpersonal skills for successful school principals when he writes, ". . . Principals require strong interpersonal skills to be successful in their schools. We know from two national studies of effective principals that they must be competent with people, all kinds of people" (p. 2). The competent principal interacts, talks, consoles, listens, cheers, advises, hugs (selectively), cries, and occasionally reprimands when required. These behaviors must be consistent, deeply felt, and honest if you, the principal, are to be the kind of servant leader needed for the postmodern school for the year 2000. Teachers and others on your staff come to work with worries about their own children, their marriages, their financial status, their health, their fear of some students, and a feeling of not being able to teach all children Given the intensity of the modern school and the diverse demands that are placed on teachers, the typical school working environment is not conducive to meeting all of their unmet needs.

Carl Glickman and Edward Pajak (1983) claim that the current organizational patterns of the school workplace inhibit interpersonal sensitivity of the entire staff. Factory-like routine, caused by policy and administrative directives, rule, and regiments the lives of teachers and staff much like factory workers. These rigid rule-bound schools promote isolation of teachers from other teachers who are stressed by teaching five or six classes and coping with mandated testing, paper work, vocal and abusive parents, and an increasing number of disruptive students.

Sensitive principals are aware of these workplace dilemmas and try to alter their schools from routine, noninspiring places where the work is drudgery to joyful centers of learning. Principals who are learning the new leadership strategies to empower and challenge the intellect and create an inner glow of professional well-being within each teacher and staff member will not only find fulfillment in their life's work but will witness successful and satisfied people. Schools must have creative, sensitive principals who share power, knowledge, praise, resources and smiles. Research tells us over and over again that the inspired teacher is one who feels respected, trusted, and involved in decisions about the school, the curriculum, the students, the teaching schedule, personal career choices, and professional development. Principals who strive to strengthen their interpersonal sensitivity toward other adults in the school and teach by example the skills of collaboration, delegation, job enrichment, and team building will become "heroes or heroines" who can mix a magic blend of leadership and followership which will result in high performance for kids and staff.

SCENARIO #3:
A PARENT AND TEACHER GRADING SQUABBLE

One of the most difficult situations for a principal is when a parent complains and upon investigation, it is apparent the teacher has not used good judgment. The problem is how to correct the problem and have the teacher maintain dignity.

One morning, a middle school principal received a phone call from a distraught parent. The parent unfolded the story about a notebook grade her son had received in a gifted and talented math class. According to the mother, 5 points per page were deducted for the lack of the student's name on each page of the notebook. Her first question was whether the district policy or procedure allowed for notebook grades to count as test grades. Second, she wanted to know the grading policy and how grades are assigned. In discussing the situation, she finally agreed that her main concern was the grade in math being affected by this notebook grade. The grade on the notebook was a 95, but with the five points per page deduction the grade became a 55. At this point the principal expressed what he heard in the parent's concern. She agreed that he had captured the nature of the complaint. The principal then told the parent that he would talk to the teacher to see if he had all the necessary information relating to this situation and that he would call her back.

In analyzing the problem, several issues had to be addressed. First, is the information from the parent accurate and complete? Second, were any district policies or procedures violated? Third, was the action by the teacher instructionally sound? Fourth, what was the nature of the evaluation and was it appropriate? Fifth, was the action by the teacher reasonable? Finally, what would be the impact on each of the parties of whatever decision was made?

In visiting with the teacher, the principal found that indeed 5 points for no name on the paper were deducted from the notebook grade. He also found that the students had been instructed on several occasions to make sure their names were on each page. The evidence in terms of the teacher's expectations and what the parent understood were consistent.

A review of both district and school policies and procedures showed that none were violated. The notebook was an acceptable assignment and was a long-standing method of evaluating students. It could be counted as a major grade.

Much can be debated over the instructional use and grading of notebooks. The primary question raised by the parent was what was being graded and to what degree. The parent contended that a penalty for not following instructions was appropriate but not of the magnitude to fail the child on that one issue. The teacher contended the penalty was justified. There was no question by either party as to the grading of the work contained in the notebook.

Was the action by the teacher reasonable? Herein lies the rub. The parent didn't think so and the teacher did.

If the teacher was supported, then the parent and student would feel that the teacher was unfair. They would also perceive that the school system had not responded to their needs. If the decisions were reversed, the teacher would lose face and the integrity of teacher grades could be compromised. Also teacher confidence in the administration could be in jeopardy. This could also spread to the entire faculty.

Was the teacher's decision reasonable? The parent claimed it was not because it was only measuring how well a student could follow instructions. It in no way indicated accomplishments in math. The teacher felt that it was reasonable because students had been warned prior to the grade being given.

The principal's dilemma was to do what he felt was right while satisfying everyone involved. On an educational level, he could not support the severity of the grade. How, then, could he support the teacher and still do what was in the overall best interest of the teacher? The only way was either to get the teacher to change his position or manipulate the situation so that the teacher got the credit for reevaluating the grading procedure. The teacher was unwilling to change his position. Therefore, the principal told the teacher to regrade the notebook deducting a maximum of 10 points for not following instructions. The principal expressed to him that he felt the parents of the students would see him as being fair, flexible, and empathetic. He also told him the parents would think highly of him. Although the teacher reluctantly agreed to what the principal asked, he still insisted his position was justified, and he commented on not being supported by the principal. The principal called the parent and told her of the decision, but he gave the teacher the credit. Two days later the teacher came by and told the principal he had several phone calls thanking him for his understanding and complimenting him on his teaching. He apologized for the negative comments and admitted that the situation was handled correctly.

WORKING WITH OTHERS

How do principals work with other adults who frequently "do their own thing" or become uncooperative and refuse to adopt new ideas or programs. One principal said, "I have some teachers who have Mayflower attitudes and are old enough to have made the voyage." Other principals just don't understand why teachers and staff dig in their collective heels and refuse to consider new ideas. It could be that the principal believes that she/he has the interpersonal sensitivity of Mother Teresa, but actually treats others like Atilla the Hun. The head and the heart are not always in synch. We cannot see in ourselves what others see. The Scottish poet Robert Burns wrote, ". . . Oh, would some power the gifty gie us, to see ourselves as others see us. . . . " We all deceive ourselves about how we are perceived by others, especially those who observe us on a regular basis. We all tend to talk one way and act another. We claim that we value and believe in our staffs but turn around and psychologically "drop kick" them to get things done. We talk about applying the humanizing elements of Theory Y but apply the dictator tactics of Theory X. Why do we do that? We tell the world that we trust people and state that they can enjoy their work as much as play, but then we watch them to make sure that they do it our way. We and the Charles Shultz character, Snoopy, know better. Snoopy says that, "A watched supper dish never fills." How often have we said, "I knew they couldn't be trusted; I should have done it myself." If we remain cynical about the motives and abilities of others on our staff, we fail to lead them in accomplishing school goals. Perhaps it all starts with having respect and love for ourselves—flaws and all—and forgiving ourselves for past acts of omission and commission. If we can do that, then maybe we can look for the best in others around us. We need to be fully aware that our interpersonal communications send clear signals about how much we trust and believe in others in the building. A high level of faith and belief in the talents and motives of others are basic to moving schools toward places where caring and learning go hand-in-hand. One way to stay on top of staff interpersonal sensitivity is frequent use of a staff sensitivity questionnaire. The Staff Sensitivity Scale in Table 3.1 is designed for principals to use with their staffs.

Perhaps the self-report data you as principal gather from this instrument can be a first step in becoming the kind of leader you want to be. Administer the instrument twice each year to keep abreast of any changes in staff perceptions about your interpersonal skill level. You can become a sensitive and visionary leader who inspires and lifts all who enter your world.

TEAM-BUILDING

The following story is an example of how teamwork saved a principal and changed a school for good. After serving as a high school principal for several years in a large suburban school district, Betty's school had been labeled a "low performer" by the State Department of Education. During the last 5 years, the student body changed form middle income and Anglo to lower income and multicultural. This rapid change carried with it a substantial drop in student test scores and in student attendance.

The superintendent, the board of education, and parents received the bad news, and pressure on the principal mounted. The superintendent told the principal to lead the school "out of the valley of low performance or else!"

Rather than make excuses for the problems that caused the low performance, the principal accepted the challenge to "turn the school performance around." After long hours of analyzing student test scores by disaggregating the data by grade, subject, and teacher, she held a 2-day retreat in July with her assistant

TABLE 3.1. STAFF SENSITIVITY SCALE
JOHN R. HOYLE, TEXAS A&M UNIVERSITY

How often does your principal—	Frequently	Occasionally	Rarely	Never
Listen to you?				
Laugh with you?				
Praise your accomplishments?				
Delegate an important task to you?				
Ignore you?				
Ask about your family, etc.?				
Discuss your career goals?				
Solve classroom student problems?				
Criticize you in front of others?				
Set high standards for students?				
Set high standards for teachers?				
Acquire needed supplies?				
Help you improve your performance?				
Give encouragement when you need it?				
Help you with parent complaints?				
Accurately evaluate your performance?				
Inaccurately evaluate your performance?				
Provide helpful staff development?				

How often does your principal—	Frequently	Occasionally	Rarely	Never
Appear tactful and caring?				
Respect culture and gender sensitivity?				
Back you up if you are right?				
Communicate clearly?				
Treat you with respect?				
Keep the building clean?				
Keep the building safe?				
Keep to him/herself?				
Share power?				
Appear unhappy?				
Make you feel important?				
Share in your victories and defeats?				
Care for you as a unique person?				
Appear too serious?				
Appear insensitive to other ethnic groups?				
Appear driven by school policies, not what's best?				
Show love for all kids?				
Inspire you to be "be better than you were before"?				
Keep his/her word?				
Keep what you say confidential?				
Appear to be a "servant-leader"?				

principal and department heads. Together they developed a vision statement and four specific goals, which included steps to reach each of the goals. In August, before students were in session, they shared the visions and goals with faculty in a small group setting over a 5-day period. This deliberate team-building process created a shared vision of a high performing school. The vision statement, "Striving to be the best as individuals and together at Wilson High School" helped unite the school faculty to join the challenge to "turn the school around." The test results and student attendance improved substantially by early spring of the school year. Betty's commitment to persist under difficult circumstances made Wilson High School a strong, caring, learning community.

A team is a group of people who function as one in pursuit of a common purpose. Being able to do this means that team members are sensitive to each other's needs, that they understand each other's strengths and weaknesses, and that they are willing to give more of themselves to achieve a mutual benefit. The common purpose of the professional staff in a school—principal, teachers, counselors, and others—is the education and emotional health of children.

Principals are the primary team builders in most schools. Most principals have been on athletic teams, in bands, or on debate teams, and they know the value of teamwork and the synergy created when a team works as a unit to win a game or contest. Often the team or unit accomplishes a victory that seemed beyond its grasp because it rose to the occasion. Remember the impossible victory in the 1980 Winter Olympics by the USA ice hockey team? We were ranked far down the list behind such world powers as the USSR, Finland, and others. Individually, the members of that USA team would not have made the first team of these tradition-rich national teams and they knew that when they started their long grueling practice sessions. America was never prouder of any victory than the Gold Medal finish over the USSR. A team of virtually unknown players knew that the word team did not include the letter "I" and became an unselfish unit to accomplish an impossible victory. Teams can move mountains that individuals only dream about.

Schools are not ice rinks, but the playing surface is similar. Slick with unsure expectations by the district, parents, and the principal; hard, with the challenge of teaching learning-disabled students and being told to "teach to the test"; cold, with no effort made to help new and veteran teachers and staff create warm friendships in the building; and frightened by fear of bodily harm from violent students or others who hang around the campus. Teams of teachers and staff are vital if schools are to succeed in a time of more students with more problems, less funding, and more political pressures from extremist groups and a seemingly unforgiving public.

Susan Clark (1995) believes that the principals hold the key to building winning school staff teams. She asserts that, "... Today, success requires the knowledge of all the professionals in the building and the community resources outside the building. The smart administrator knows that to tap into that collective wisdom, a team must be forged" (p. 9). The smart principal also knows that team-building takes time and patience. Working in teams is not a natural behavior for most of us. We come into the world crying "me, me, me," and struggle the rest of our lives trying to share our lives with others who are also self centered. Team work is anathema to our makeup, even though social scientists claim that we are social animals who need each other. Perhaps the reason that forming and developing successful teams is so difficult is that most teams are merely groups that have little focus and limited power to change things for the better.

Teamwork is good! Everyone is doing it. Leaders of the future will be those who are highly specialized and can lead teams of specialists. Team membership skills can be taught by the schools. Education researchers tell us that cooperative learning is working for kids and that peer-assisted learning is a must to boost student achievement. However, school staffs continue to stumble along using the "team" or site-based decision making models with mixed results. Teachers and other staff need quality staff development to learn team skills and collaboration. The principal must use his or her interpersonal sensitivity skills to lead the way as a team oriented learner. The principal is responsible to see that the training is conducted and to be an active participant in the training.

SCENARIO #4:
THE BLOCK SCHEDULE CHANGE AND PATIENCE

Sensitivity with faculty and staff directly relates to the culture and climate of the school. How a principal relates in a group setting will set the tone for the building. Therefore, a positive, collegial climate should be a goal of every principal.

Change is always difficult. The situation in which one principal found herself was a setup for a failure. She had opened a new school with new faculty and students from three different schools. The school had opened with eighth and ninth grades. Two years later, the school had gone to grades six though eight. Now, 1 year later, they were going to implement an alternating block schedule. Drastic change seemed to be the norm. In opening the school and trying to create a team with the faculty from various campuses, several mistakes were made and they had a tough year. The next year was better. The year with sixth through eighth grades added new staff, but overall was a stable year. The district implemented a formal site-based decision-making procedure. The principal had always operated a site-based decision-making model, but a formal process was put into place district wide which was also more in-depth that what had been used. The new process required more change.

The Building Leadership Team (BLT) decided that different scheduling patterns should be researched because of a need identified through the previous year's evaluation. Students were too limited in what subjects they could take.

The BLT researched scheduling patterns and decided on two for additional study. These two addressed the needs of the students and were compatible with the mission statement of the school. Teams of teachers and parents went to sites to observe the patterns being studied. The one which was selected was the alternating block schedule. This would cause the teacher to have 90-minute classes instead of the usual 55 minutes. Yet another change!

The problem the principal faced was how to implement change while being sensitive to the needs of the faculty and staff. Too much too quickly equals failure. Sensitivity to the frustration point of the faculty was essential. Even though she worked through the BLT, care had to be taken not to overload the teacher.

It became clear that the change to 90 minutes was causing concern among the faculty. The problem was how to address this concern without creating the teacher frustration of being overloaded with work in the form of staff development. Therefore, a plan for utilizing strategies of collaboration, shared problem solving, assessing student progress, and administrative support was developed.

The implementation of the plan was carefully monitored in order to identify levels of frustration of the faculty. What do you look for when trying to determine how a faculty feels? First, you need to watch for signs of fatigue. Physical appearance is the first symptom. Other symptoms include late arriving, early leaving, missing duty, more discipline referrals, and negative conversations regarding student motivation, student ability, or administrative support. In looking for these indicators, a principal needs to determine if these are just an individual reaction, either personal or school related, to stress. All teachers at times will exhibit those symptoms. It is up to the principal to determine whether the symptoms are personal or institutional. Then, treatment will be either on a personal or institutional level. Sensitivity in identifying and reacting to personal and institutional stress is critical for success in building a positive culture.

Second, a principal needs to talk informally with the faculty. This is a time for listening and learning. Through conversations teachers will generally express their feelings. This may not be a direct criticism, but listening for the tone and substance can give you clues as to stress level. Listen for excessive emphasis on *"Thank God it's Friday, I can't wait for [the weekend, retirement, vacation/holiday plans],"* or medical complaints.

Third, classroom visits can give you clues to stress levels of the faculty. Classes being assigned worksheets at an abnormal rate, teachers sitting at their desks during instruction and the "feeling" of the class being strained are symptoms of teacher stress.

Fourth, faculty meetings can give you clues also. People being late, difficulty in getting the group focused, and petty concerns turning into major issues are a few of the tell-tale signs.

Finally, outside influences can also affect the stress level. Principals must be sensitive to community pressures that affect staff morale. A winning athletic team helps build morale. A defeated bond election can cause tension. Being alert and adjusting building programs can contribute to high staff morale.

Sensitivity of the principal to stress level will determine success or failure. If the staff shows high energy levels, concern for students, and concern for each other, capitalize on this and accelerate change. If the staff exhibits symptoms of high stress, then back off programs or at least restructure them. In any long-term project of change, both will occur.

All of the above were used in implementing the plan to establish the alternating block schedule. At first, when energy was high, the principal had after-school staff development focusing on teaching strategies for the 90-minute period. When signs of stress were exhibited, staff development was canceled, social times for faculty participation were planned, and colleague-to-colleague visits were held.

After 2 years, the alternating block was begun. It had great success because the faculty supported it. But being sensitive to faculty and staff needs throughout the process insured success.

TAKING THE "STUMBLE" OUT OF
SITE-BASED DECISION-MAKING

Unlike other school reforms that come and go, site-based decision-making is here to stay. However, if it is to be effective, much team training is necessary for the site-based team, the entire faculty, and the support staff. Principals have a difficult time finding a few minutes in each day to learn the skills to teach to others. This is like white water rafting with a broom handle paddle! While help is slowly on the way from university programs, principal academies, and school district workshops, perhaps following 10 site-based commandments (Hoyle, 1992,

November, pp. 81–87, permission granted) may help you navigate the swift currents and avoid the rocks until help arrives.

1. THOU SHALT LOOK SHARP AND FEEL SHARP

Image is important in troubled and confused times. Try to look like you have everything under control even if inside you are somewhere between butterflies and ulcers. How you appear to others is most important. The way in which you manage your daily behavior and appearance affects your ability to persuade others to share in the site-based vision and plan. By accepting your leadership position as principal, you accepted the responsibility to be a role model in the community and for the students in your school. This role model includes good health habits and high energy. To run the halls, attend meetings, chair civic and church organizations, and respond to added demands of site-based leadership, you must establish a regular exercise program to keep up appearance and energy level. When you are pleased with the condition of your body and you have a high energy level, you can place more demands on yourself without worrying about physical survival. You will have more energy to direct to the needs of others.

A sensitive school is a community where individuals are in tune with each other; but, first, each individual must be in tune with him/herself. Teachers, staff, and students admire a principal who has the self-discipline to stay fit and who encourages others to take up an exercise program. The school energy level and performance will reach a higher level in short time. Don't forget, you are being watched. Others admire the role you play and in most cases respect the tough job you do each day. You need to appear that you know where you are going and are eager to get there. Look sharp and be sharp.

2. THOU SHALT LEARN THE LANGUAGE OF EFFECTIVE TEACHING AND LEARNING

Teachers need someone at the head of their school organization who can respond to their needs in the language of their own technical expertise. Teachers respect well-read, intelligent leaders who can discuss the teaching/learning process, curriculum design, teaching strategies, student assessment, and motivation. If you are computer alert and familiar with effective uses for other learning technologies and can take over a classroom and teach, you are keeping this commandment. You cannot be an expert in all content areas, but you can be an expert coach of teachers and staff by having a grasp of classroom management, teaching models, and learning resources. If you refuse to sharpen your knowledge and language in teaching and learning, you may be viewed as an overpaid office boy in charge of "heat, light, and ventilation," who wouldn't know a noun from a pronoun if she/he/it/them hit him with a water balloon. You must speak the language of current teaching and learning to be a sensitive, site-based leader.

3. Thou Shalt Be Visible

Be where you can hear things and can respond to the needs of people inside and outside of the school. You must walk the halls, eat in the cafeteria, talk to kids, staff, visitors, teachers, and community members. You are the key ambassador for the school. Business and community leaders gain a perception of the school through the words and ideas you discuss with them. Accept the speaking opportunities at the Rotary and Lions clubs, churches, and other community groups—that comes with the territory. Being visible and interacting with others about ways to make the school better is your job and one of the reasons you like what you do—do it more often! Remember the old adage— 90% of success in life is being there when people need you. Be visible and your site-based model will be the benchmark for others.

4. Thou Shalt Train Teachers and Staff in the Art of Decision-making and Consensus Building

Show teachers that you believe they are important by truly empowering them. Most teachers, staff, and site-based teams are uncomfortable with group processes and team-building skills. You must never forget to be sensitive to the fact that most people who work in schools lead hectic lives and are exhausted after a day of teaching, counseling, nursing, cleaning, cooking, and keyboarding. They do not welcome the opportunity to sit in groups and discuss items that hold no personal interest for them.

Team-building for the sake of team-building is a morale buster. Your school staff has no burning desire to spend what little energy they have left deciding matters of little consequence to them.

Bridges (1967) identified two tests to determine when to involve others in a decision: the test of relevance and the test of expertise. If the staff has no personal stake or expertise in the decision, then it falls in their zone of acceptance. If, however, the staff has a high personal stake and expertise in the decision, they should be invited to help make the decision. Sensitive principals work with staff to arrange inservice training in the processes of decision making and consensus building. Without adequate training in group processes, staff will not actively participate in decision-making. You should immediately start training together for successful site-based management. It takes time, but research and best practice lead us to believe that the effort will pay off in higher morale and exciting student achievement.

5. THOU SHALT TELL THE TRUTH

Sensitivity is based on truth; trust is built on truth. When in doubt tell the truth. You must live with yourself first. The failure to tell the truth and be honest has ruined the careers of many school principals. If your staff is asked to accept more responsibility and make their own decisions, then they need principals with strong principles. Research studies reveal that employees place honesty as the number one attribute they want in their leader. If your word is no good, then your leadership is over. Tell the truth and when your memory fails, you will not have to worry about what you told someone. Sensitive, site-based leaders have a strong moral center which guides their daily conversations and insures that the truth is told.

6. THOU SHALT MAKE HEROES AND HEROINES OF OTHERS

Sensitive principals focus the spotlight on the achievements of teachers, other staff members, advisory council members, and students. You need to select a hero or heroine of the week, semester, and year in several categories and arrange for these success stories to appear in the local newspapers, TV, radio, and district news letter. Throw a few school parties for these stars. People need recognition from you and their peers to feel important in their chosen profession. Little things make students feel important when it happens before their peers. Harry Crenshaw, while principal of Sam Rayburn Middle School in Bryan, Texas, singled out kids with birthdays and would surprise them in the cafeteria with a resounding rendition of "Happy Birthday!" The kids always appeared to be embarrassed, but their faces would glow with the pride of recognition by their principal. Crenshaw discovered that tooting the horns of others, rather than his own, paid high dividends in morale, low absenteeism, and student achievement. His philosophy is to praise much, ignore a lot; in other words, "brag, don't nag." A family atmosphere where praise and recognition are plentiful and targeted will produce motivated winners and is a morale booster for everyone in the school. It is true that when you pat someone on the back, their head seems to swell with pride. Site-based teams will spread the glory of success as a result of your pats on backs.

7. THOU SHALT HAVE HIGH EXPECTATIONS

The sensitive principal recognizes the potential for success in other people, even when they fail to see it themselves. When you expect the best, you very often get it. A former professor at Texas A&M University, Paul Hensarling, told all of his advisees to be "better than you think you can be." Success begets success in our journey in life. Once we find success in achieving a very difficult goal, the next goal becomes achievable Our personal vision of success is often clouded by some limitation that we ourselves or someone else has planted in our minds. An old track coach told his fallen hurdler that, "the hurdles in your mind are much higher than those on the track—get up and get over them one at a time." John Hoyle finds that many current and future school leaders have a fear of success. They are so unsure of their abilities that they do not apply for the big jobs. They say, "But, Dr. Hoyle, I watch the person in that job and I don't believe that I can handle all of that pressure and detail. That is such a visible position and I would be afraid of failure and lose my good reputation." Hoyle's reaction is to tell these fearful students that they should take a run at the position they fear. Why on earth would these students pay the high price to earn a graduate degree unless they were seeking to rise to a position of influence in education? There is much truth to the old saying, "If you think you can or you can't, you are right either way." Sensitive school principals tell all who will listen about the magic link between good luck and hard work. It is amazing to some that lucky successful people are usually the hardest workers. Your hard work and positive expectations for yourself and others in the school can work wonders. Keep modeling and telling your staff that down deep inside of themselves is the power to succeed and that is what you expect from them. The taste of sour lemons pounds you each day in your difficult role as principal. Your task is to sprinkle the sugar of praise on your students, staff, and faculty and share the lemonade of success. Site-based decision-making is much sweeter when you, the leader, are generous with the sugar.

8. THOU SHALT EVALUATE PERFORMANCE

Almost all teachers want to do their best. An appraisal system that is responsive to their needs will enable them to do this. Sensitive principals are aware that performance appraisals strikes fear in the hearts of all who are undergoing evaluation. We want to know how we are doing, but the realties of the "boss" evaluating our work is daunting to say the least. However, if students are our top priority, then the system that educates them needs constant appraisal. How then can the staff evaluation process be less painful and help staff members be "better than they can be."

First—Rethink the school vision statement. Conduct a visioning workshop for all faculty and staff to take another look at the school vision statement. Does the statement drive the energies of everyone to a higher level of success and hope for the future? Does it have a "target that beckons" each person to pull together for the welfare of the kids? Rework the words until the vision is clear, compelling, bought by everyone.

Second—Ask each staff member to write five or six specific goals directly related to the vision statement and indicators or activities that he or she will use to facilitate the accomplishment of each goal.

Third—Schedule a 30-minute meeting with each staff member to share the goals and indicators and to alter them if necessary. During this meeting brag on the abilities of each person and tell them that the goals will be reached and that you will assist them in that success through targeted inservice and mentoring from others. Tell them that the students are our reason for being and that together we will succeed far beyond the goals we have written.

Fourth—Frequently pop in and out of classrooms and staff workplaces to observe. After a time the fear of you being viewed as a "snoopervisor" will diminish because of your regular visits. There is nothing in the research that requires three, four, or five observation periods for evaluators. Trust and respect are the twins of victory in making staff evaluation a positive part of any winning school team.

Five—Schedule a 30-minute session with each staff member to ask them how well he or she reached each goal for the year thus far. Next, brag on the successes and the creative strategies used to reach the targets. Close with suggestions to helpthe staff memeber be even better the next evaluation period. Tell them how proud you are of them and quote basketball coach Pat Riley: ". . . Anytime you stop trying to get better, you're bound to get worse." Tell them to keep the vision for kids, and the school will be the best ever. Evaluation and clear benchmarks are vital to the decisions made by the site-based team to help set higher and more appropriate goals for kids.

9. THOU SHALT KEEP A SENSE OF HUMOR

Interpersonal sensitivity requires an ability to put things in perspective, to not take oneself too seriously. A sense of humor enables this, and it provides a vehicle for the principal to reach out and welcome others into the partnership of running the school.

"Laughers last," according to the mental health experts. Several years ago Norman Cousins, a well-known writer and scholar, was diagnosed with a terminal illness. Rather than give in to the gloomy prognosis, he decided to heed some little-known evidence that laughter had the power to heal. Cousins began viewing movies of Laurel and Hardy, Charlie Chaplin, the Three Stooges, and others that made him belly laugh. His health improved greatly and his life became even richer than before. He became a visiting professor of humor in medicine at a major research and teaching hospital, and through laughter therapy helped hundreds of terminally ill patients extend their lives. Cousins wrote a book about his success with laughter for healing titled *The Anatomy of an Illness*.

A keen sense of humor is a vital tool to help you and the staff ride the waves of stress and some failure. A sincere smile, a silly pun, or a good funny story can lighten the burdens of a staff. A smile can "lift the gloom in the room." It is true that it takes more muscles to frown than to smile, and, as a result, unhappy people may be working themselves to death. Laugh a lot, smile a lot, and watch the faces light up when you come near. Sensitive site-based leaders need humor to lighten the load they carry for the staff and the kids.

10. THOU SHALT BE A DREAM KEEPER

Researchers are discovering what we knew, that charismatic visionaries inspire others to work harder, longer hours, and outperform workers who labor under traditional managers. The staff of a school must be driven by a vision of their school of the future where all kids are successful and good citizens. Your own vision should be compelling and your skills to persuade others to help you build the school vision must be honed to a fine edge. Your enthusiasm can lead the staff to create a "field of dreams" which will attract others to your learning community.

Above all, keep in mind that while you are "keeping" the dream, it is not yours alone. You are holding it in trust for others—particularly your staff. The vision you keep must be the vision of others also. If you really value the vision that is being created and if you invite others to help build and shape it, you are saying to them that they are important. In doing this you will be responding to some of their deepest personal needs and concerns—the first element in our definition of interpersonal sensitivity.

Write a scenario about your school for the future and share it with the staff. Follow this with a workshop and create groups of six to eight people to discuss the scenario and the steps needed to make the dream come true. Also find ways to overcome the barriers that could kill the dream. Stephen Covey (1990) calls us to "keep the end in mind" when we look to a positive future. Always talk in terms of the future successes. For example: It is now 2005 and we are in our virtual reality school viewing the rain forests of the Amazon. Our students are linked to the super electronic highway and are communicating with students throughout the world about environmental issues important to the future of the planet. Teachers are assisting the students with new data and encouraging them to ask higher order questions about the environment. This ability to dream and inspire others to help build the vision is not only motivational but can help a stressed staff look beyond daily struggles and keep an eye on tomorrow. Walt Disney said, "If you can dream it, you can do it."

Following these 10 commandments will help you look for the best in yourself and in others. Viktor Frankl (1967), writing about his horrible 3 years as a prisoner of the Nazis at Auschwitz, concluded that he and others who survived knew the "why" of life. He surmised that if a person has a compelling expectation in his life (i.e., seeing his child again or finishing a rare manuscript or project), he can stay alive and survive under the most inhumane conditions of the camp. Frankl wrote, ". . . He knows the 'why' for his existence and will be able to bear almost any 'how'" (p. 127). Try to apply these basic commandments and observe the changes in your own attitude and the morale of the staff. Don't forget the "why" in your life and the "why" in the lives of others. This "why" is the cause beyond ourselves which makes life worth living and our professional roles meaningful.

CONCLUSION

Interpersonal sensitivity toward your teachers and other staff members is a continuous pursuit. The pressures of the job and the stress of constant change can cause you as principal to "hole up" and hide from the world. This evasive action is directly opposite to the behaviors you need to reveal to your staff members who need your calm, steady, optimistic, and energetic presence. When a teacher is upset, angry, or frustrated, the last thing needed is an insensitive leader. You as principal are not "one of the gang" and you cannot lead if you fall victim to your feelings of despair and frustration. You are the one who tells others, "I am sorry about your problem, but together we can solve it because we have the talent and heart to do the right things for each other and for the students." Research tells us that leaders who are sensitive to the feelings of others and try to help them through their problems have high "emotional intelligence." Daniel Goleman (1995) believes that the smartest people are not always the most successful because they may fail to read the feelings of others. He calls "people skills," such as empathy and other skills in reading the social situation, the reason why some leaders who lack sheer raw intelligence rise to the top of their professions. According to Nancy Gibbs, in a report in *Time* magazine (October 2, 1995, p. 66), ". . . IQ gets you hired, but EQ (emotional intelligence) gets you promoted." Gibbs reports that workers who are good collaborators and networkers and popular with colleagues are more likely to get the cooperation they need to reach their goals than are socially awkward geniuses.

Principals who can keep their cool and lead others through the stresses of long, frustrating, school days and years, and build their interpersonal skills of empathy, collaboration, listening, handling anger, frustration, and criticism will move a school staff and its students to higher morale and performance. Emotion is more important than facts to most of us. Reading and acting on the feelings of others are gifts that can pay major benefits in places we call schools. Use the Staff Sensitivity Scale and follow the 10 site-based commandments and you will be two steps closer to becoming a sensitive leader.

SKILL BUILDING ACTIVITIES

1. Use the following checklist to assess yourself in terms of the Ten Commandments.

   A. What steps are you taking to look sharp and feel sharp?

	Yes	No
♦ Exercise program.	____	____
♦ Regular physicals.	____	____
♦ Healthy diet.	____	____
♦ Adequate rest.	____	____
♦ Professional wardrobe.	____	____
♦ Healthy lifestyle.	____	____

   B. Are you learning the language of effective teaching and learning?

	Yes	No
♦ Learning styles.	____	____
♦ Teaching strategies, i.e., cooperative learning, mastery teaching, etc.	____	____
♦ Alternative assessments.	____	____
♦ Student motivation.	____	____
♦ Student motivation activities.	____	____
♦ Computer-based teaching.	____	____
♦ CD-ROM and other electronic teaching processes.	____	____

   C. Are you staying visible?

	Yes	No
♦ In the hallways?	____	____
♦ In the classrooms?	____	____
♦ At athletic and other student events?	____	____
♦ At important community functions?	____	____

- In a civic club?   ____   ____
- In a church or synagogue?   ____   ____
- Among business people?   ____   ____
- With your family?   ____   ____

D. How are you training teachers and staff in the art of decision-making and consensus building?

	Yes	No
Conduct training yourself.	____	____
Bring outside trainers.	____	____
Plan regular (3–4 times a year) training.	____	____
Plan with others the best time for the training.	____	____
Apply the tests of relevance and expertise before involving others.	____	____
Model consensus building and shared decision-making.	____	____

E. Do you tell the truth on

	Yes	No
Budget matters?	____	____
Student matters?	____	____
Teacher matters?	____	____
Staff evaluation matters?	____	____
Personal matters?	____	____

F. How do you make heroes and heroines of others?

	Yes	No
Recognize their achievements in front of peers.	____	____
Thank them personally for outstanding performance.	____	____

- Write congratulatory letters
  or cards to staff and students. _____   _____

G. Do you hold high expectations for

	Yes	No
Student academic perfor-mance?	_____	_____
Student behavior?	_____	_____
Teacher performance?	_____	_____
Staff performance?	_____	_____
Self-performance?	_____	_____

H. What evaluation processes do you use?

	Yes	No
Share in building a school vision.	_____	_____
Ask teachers and staff to write five or six specific goals.	_____	_____
You or your designee meets with each staff member to share the goals and discuss them.	_____	_____
Observe the teachers and staff members on a regular basis.	_____	_____
You or your designee meet with each teacher and staff member to discuss their successes and areas of improvement.	_____	_____
Make positive and sensitive suggestions to help each employee improve each year.	_____	_____

I. Do you use humor frequently with

	Yes	No
◆ Students?	___	___
◆ Teachers?	___	___
◆ Staff?	___	___
◆ Parents?	___	___
◆ Yourself?	___	___

J. How do you keep the school dream alive?

	Yes	No
◆ Constantly sharing your vision with others.	___	___
◆ Asking teachers and staff to share their vision for the school.	___	___
◆ Inviting students to write scenarios about their school in 2005.	___	___
◆ Including parents and other community members in the dream building process.	___	___

2. Use the Staff Sensitivity Scale (Table 3.1) with a group of teachers to assess your sensitivity to their needs. (If you are not currently a principal, many of the items will not be applicable. However, a number will be pertinent, and you can use them to assess your likely future performance as a principal.) Use your assessment as a guide for building your interpersonal sensitivity skills.

4

BEING SENSITIVE TO PARENTS AND OTHERS IN THE COMMUNITY

Parents and other community members need principals who are sensitive to their feelings even though these feelings may run counter to what principals believe that need or want from them. You as a principal need to put yourself inside the skin of other people in order to be sensitive to the needs and pressures that cause them to act in various ways.

A principal of a school in South Texas found out the difference between promoting parent involvement in the life of her school and the reality of being a parent. The principal was deeply concerned about 13-year-old Armando's frequent absences from school and decided to go visit Armando's parents to discuss the problem. The principal had difficulty finding the house in the barrio section of town. Using her limited Spanish, she was directed to a small tarpaper shack where Armando's family lived. Entering the grassless, dusty, yard, the principal was warmly greeted by Armando's father who invited her inside. She sat on an old plastic couch and asked why Armando was absent so much from school. The father told her that Armando was the oldest of their seven children and was needed to help him work in the fields to pick vegetables and fruit because this work provided enough money for the family to survive. With tear-filled eyes, the father then promised that Armando would improve his attendance, because his education was the most important goal for Armando's future. The principal was pleased with the promise made by the father and the expression of his love and concern for Armando and his future.

Three months passed and Armando had perfect attendance and was improving his grades. And then it happened—Armando was gone. The principal found an empty tarpaper house. According to a neighbor the father took the family to Michigan to work on a farm for migrant workers. Rather than becoming angry at the father's broken promises, the sensitive principal cried. She cried for Armando and his family. She cried because she feared that Armando's life would never be better than his father's, and that the school had lost a precious student from its family.

From this experience with Armando, the principal learned a valuable lesson. She learned that if she was going to truly serve the students of her community, she needed to find out the needs of the families first. If acts of sensitivity truly took priority in her interpersonal relationships, then parents and community members would be more prone to help her in serving the school and its needs. If Armando wants to enroll in her school when the harvest is over, the principal will welcome him and his father with an open heart.

SENSITIVITY TO THE NEEDS OF PARENTS

Sensitivity to the needs of parents/guardians is the first step in getting them involved in school activities. Parent/guardian involvement in the school is the primary factor in effective schools. Parents who express interest in the school curriculum, teaching methods, and other instruction related activities usually have kids who achieve well academically and socially. Anne T. Henderson summarized nearly 50 studies of parental involvement. She concluded:

> Programs designed with strong parent involvement produce students who perform better than otherwise identical programs that do not involve parents as thoroughly, or that do not involve them at all. Schools

that relate well to their communities have student bodies that outperform other schools. Children whose parents help them at home and stay in touch with the school score higher than children of similar aptitudes and family background whose parents are not involved. Schools where children are failing improve dramatically when parents are called in to help (Amundson, 1988, p. 82).

The literature is full of ideas on ways to get more parents involved in their children's schooling. The most common approaches are sending notices home with the kids or by mail. Some schools use a PTO telephone tree to contact parents about events and volunteer opportunities. Parents Day, Grandparents Day, family spaghetti dinners, and open houses are typical and successful tactics to attract parents to the school and classrooms.

Another strategy to attract parents is the parent-teacher conference for every child. This approach is usually very successful in middle- and upper-class schools, where one parent is at home or employed as a professional and can take time to meet with the teacher. In lower-income homes where both parents or a single parent lacks the transportation and cannot take off from work during the day, parent-teacher conferences may not take place. Also, these parents may work long hours and hold two jobs which makes it impossible to attend regularly scheduled conferences. As in Armando's family, these economic conditions for many parents often negatively impact teacher-parent communication about the progress of the child. Unthinking teachers and principals can become insensitive to these conditions of economic survival that exist for some families and cast aspersions at these parents because of their "lack of interest in their children."

What, then, can you and the staff do to become more sensitive to the real needs and pressures parents face and to encourage their involvement in the school? How can you develop greater sensitivity to the work and family patterns of those you serve? The following ideas may reinforce what you are now doing, or perhaps you may find a helpful hint to help your school "be better than you think it can be."

ESTABLISH "TALK WITH THE PRINCIPAL" SESSIONS

Once a week invite three to five parents to school for lunch. After the parents and students enjoy a quick lunch together, dismiss the children and then you and the parents can talk about issues facing their kids and the school. While this forum may not be appropriate to discuss some of the more problematic concerns, i.e., disciplinary action, etc., parents will view you as a communicator who really cares about their children and themselves. When the more serious concerns surface in the group discussions, invite the parent to come back for a personal conference. Lowell Strike, a principal in Bryan, Texas, conducts weekly "coffee talks" in various neighborhoods. A parent will open his/her home and invite other parents to share ideas with Strike and each other. He finds these sessions very informational, and they help him understand the social and community cultures as he gets to know parents on a first name basis. These informal coffee talks have helped Lowell Strike to increase his sensitivity and to anticipate problems before they occur. They give him greater insights into the feelings, hopes, and desires of those he serves.

Another traditional, but very successful, way to encourage parents to meet and talk with you is a biweekly "Meet the Principal Night." This forum should be a very informal and free-flowing discussion about ways to help each child succeed. A nice touch that one of the authors uses is to create a drawing of a "Generic Kid" and make a transparency or draw it on a flip chart or blackboard. The "Generic Kid" is a big round circle face with two big round eyes, a big silly grin, and a curly prig of hair on top. Underneath place the words "Generic Kid." When the discussion gets a little intense remind the parent(s) that you have come together to help each "kid" become a successful, happy, and moral young leader. You may begin the session with these words: "I am very pleased that you have taken your time this evening to talk about your most precious gift—your child." While pointing to the "Generic Kid" say: "As we discuss ways to help your child become more successful in school and as a person, let's remember to keep our focus on the child and not on us or our personal problems." These words tend to work miracles by keeping personal agendas under control and directing the conversations toward ways to really help each child in the school.

Regular open house nights can be very successful if parents really feel needed and have transportation to the school. College Station, Texas, Junior High School has a "Parent-to-Parent" program which includes sending busses into low-income neighborhoods to bring parents to an open house to meet the teachers and other parents. Parents who attend are offered small group sessions on several topics of interest, e.g., peer pressure, study skills, social acceptance, and self-esteem. The principal, teachers, assistant principals, and counselors find these sessions help them gain greater sensitivity to the needs of these parents and families.

In spite of bussing services, attendance by lower-income parents at open house nights is still likely to remain low if the school's attendance zone covers several distinct neighborhoods. If this is the case, the school needs to explore alternatives that will allow the principal and teachers to meet the parents on their own turf. The next two recommendations illustrate ways of doing this.

CREATE RELIGIOUS INSTITUTION FORUMS CALLED "MEET YOUR SCHOOL PRINCIPAL"

Contact local religious leaders about setting up these sessions. The best way to begin is to meet with the local ministerial alliance. This is an excellent forum to meet most of the religious leaders who can be very influential allies to help you with community, parent, and student problems and issues. Most of these ministers will welcome you into their places of worship to hold discussions with members about the schools and their children. Also, they can provide vital information about the families and their struggles to help their children. As mentioned earlier, Jonathon Kozol's book, *Amazing Grace*, focuses on religious institutions and leaders as powerful agents for making schools more caring and successful places for kids. Build strong ties with these spiritual and community leaders, and your job as principal will be lifted by a group of people who really do have a "cause beyond themselves." This "cause" should be the main reason that keeps you in your role as principal.

"MEET THE PRINCIPAL AT YOUR WORK PLACE"

"Meet the principal at your work place" is another suggestion that may help. Through a random process select two parents a week to visit at their work sites. Call them and find out if you can see them for a few minutes to talk about their child and the school. Keep the visits short and positive and encourage the parents to come to school for open houses and "Meet Your Child's Teacher Night." This effort to meet parents at their work site demonstrates your sensitivity to their children and your willingness to help them as individuals. This happened in Indianapolis, Indiana, when the schools and the business community created a Parents-In-Touch program to attract every parent to attend parent-teacher conferences held twice a year. Businesses spread the word to encourage employers to release their employees to attend the conferences. The schools then arranged their conference schedules around the parents' available time.

IMPROVING PARENT-PRINCIPAL COMMUNICATIONS

When meeting with parents in face-to-face settings the right kinds of messages must be sent when you speak. You need to have clear goals in mind and replay your mind tapes several times before you say the wrong things which could possibly embarrass, intimidate or anger a parent. Joyce Epstein (1995) believes that educators are not always well-trained in becoming good communicators with parents. She states that, "Just about all teachers and administrators would like to involve families, but many do not know how to go about building positive and productive programs and consequently are fearful about trying. This creates a "rhetoric rut," in which educators are stuck, expressing support for partnerships without taking any action (p. 703). With this caveat in mind, you as school principal need to build your communication skills in the following ways:

♦ Respect all parents as caring partners to help you help their child.

♦ Make yourself accessible to parents who have limited time to talk with you.

♦ Continue to tell all parents that your school needs them to get more involved in all parts of the school life.

♦ Respect the values, customs, and language differences and improve your communication skills on a continuing basis.

Parents need you as principal to be sensitive to their fears for the future of their children and youth. If you show through your actions and words that their child is your first concern, parents will drop their fears and communicate openly with you and the staff and become true partners in the battle for the long struggle to success for their child.

Scenario #5: "Hooky" and Hot Parents

One Friday a field trip was planned for all the students who made the honor roll. The trip was a reward for their hard work during the 6-week grading period. Upon returning from their trip, teachers instructed the students to return to their third period class. It was just prior to the lunch period. Three young ladies decided not to go back to class and wait for lunch. Since the school had three lunch periods, the girls visited with friends and ate during all three lunches, effectively skipping third period. They were caught. Their excuse was that they thought they were excused from class because of the field trip and didn't realize they were to go back to class. On other field trips when they returned during their lunch, they had been excused from class. Since they had returned prior to lunch, they were instructed to go to class, but they claimed they had not heard the teacher's instructions. A check with the teacher revealed that clear instructions had been given. Therefore, the students had "cut" class. The consequence of this offense was assignment to the in-school suspension room. All parents were called and messages left on their answering machines. Problem solved.

Friday night should be a time to relax. Not true on this night. All the girls involved were leaders at school. They had never been referred to the office and only had minor classroom infractions. One of the girl's parents and the principal had been in high school together. Another girl involved was the daughter of a prominent attorney whose wife was an officer in the P.T.O. The third girl's parents were very active in the community. The phone began to ring. From the calls, the principal knew the parents had already talked to each other. They all attacked the situation from two points of view. First, they defended the girls saying that previous trips had allowed them to go to lunch without going to class. Second, that their rights were violated in that the assistant principal didn't allow the students to explain their position. After visiting with each parent, it was apparent that there was something more going on than just a reaction to kids playing hooky. The parents, together, wanted to meet with the principal on Monday morning.

Monday morning, the principal had the meeting requested by the parents. In the meantime, he had checked with the teacher and clarified that specific instructions to return to class had been given to the students. Also, he confirmed what instructions had been given to students on previous trips. In the past, when students had returned to school just before the third lunch, they had been allowed to wait on the bus until that lunch had begun. At the beginning of the meeting, the parents were defending their children's' actions. When the principal explained the circumstances, they agreed that the students should have gone back to class, but they began arguing the severity of the offense and that their girls were "good" and had never been in trouble. As they talked, the real issue surfaced—the parents objected to the assignment to in-school suspension and the terms "hooky" or "cutting class."

Being sensitive to parents involves trying to determine their perceptions of the school's actions based on their experience. It became apparent that to them hooky involved "troublemakers" and activities which were serious while missing school. Also, the parents thought that the term "suspension" involved negative connotations. They perceived that the in-school suspension was for incorrigibles. They didn't want their child associated with "those" kids and expressed concern about a suspension being on their permanent record.

After discovering the root of the problem, the first thing the principal needed to do was to get the parents to admit their children were at fault. The principal then rephrased the problem by indicating the students had disobeyed the teacher and had missed class. This was after an explanation of prior field trip procedures and that in-school suspension was not a suspension from school. He explained that it is an alternative educational placement. With this understanding, the parents did agree that the students should have gone to class as directed. As to the punishment he suggested that instead of the in-school suspension, that the girls could not eat with their friends for two weeks. The parents agreed that this was an appropriate punishment.

The key to the solution was defining the real problem and offering an alternative without compromising the integrity of the procedures. Any sign of catering to the influential sector of the community could be perceived by parents and students as being unfair, thereby leaving the door open to future conflicts and a loss of credibility. It also told the girls involved that when they take advantage of a situation, natural consequences will follow. There were no negative repercussions from the incident. In fact positive results were garnered in that the parents involved were complimentary of the way it was handled, as noted by comments from other parents who knew what had transpired.

IMPROVING TEACHER/PARENT CONFERENCING SKILLS

Many teachers lack the skills to be effective in parent-teacher conferences. You can assist them by not only being sensitive to this deficiency, but by offering training in this critical area. Steven Enoch (1995, November), Principal at Friday Harbor High School in Washington State, has nine strategies to help empower teachers to be confident experts in teacher-parent conferencing:

- Identify students' strengths and weaknesses in the areas of reading, writing, listening, and speaking. Teachers must have the data to alert a parent if his/her child is deficient in any of these areas and take steps to help the student overcome these deficiencies.

- Establish a clear understanding of academic areas where the student is progressing and any areas where the student is not making adequate progress. Teachers must have the skills to keep a running account of each child's progress to help them keep parents informed about the academic and social progress of each child.

- Provide parents with samples of work that reflect their child's progress. Assist teachers in learning the positive uses of portfolios for each child. Develop a rich account of a variety of each student's performance and products. Parents need to see something more than test scores and report cards to help them help their child.

- Identify the level of the student's participation and contribution to group work and cooperative assignments. What process role does the student seem most comfortable assuming? Peter Drucker and other management experts believe that the ability to be a team worker and to work cooperatively with others is a top skill for workers in the future. Parents need to know if their child can work with others and can solve problems working in a team environment. To make sure that the students have these tools for the future, the teacher needs skills in teaching group process and team-building.

- Does the child think critically and creatively? Can the student do more than merely memorize facts? Can he/she compare and contrast data and draw conclusions and create novel solutions to problems? Does the teacher help students engage in futuring exercises to help students learn skills in visioning a positive self image of success?

◆ Review the quality of the child's peer relationships for the parent. Parents need to know the kinds of friends their child associates with each day at school. Since peer influence is probably the most powerful influence on children and youth, parents need to know as much as possible about the friends and relationships of their children. Confidentiality must be maintained as much as possible between the teacher and parent on this sensitive issue. However, this information could head off serious problems for those kids who are more easily influenced than others.

◆ Identify two or three growth goals for the student. Teachers need to help parents identify two or three clear goals that they can help their child shoot for. Make certain that the parents understand the goals and what role the teacher and parent play in helping the student accomplish the goals.

◆ Provide specific expectations for what parents are to do at home to help. Teachers need to be sensitive to how much a parent can reasonably help their child at home. The more specific the instructions for helping the child, the more likely the parent will help in positive ways. Confusion on the part of the teacher and the parent about how to help at home will merely cause frustration and block parent/child communication.

◆ Take time to listen to parents about their child. What the child likes and dislikes is best known by the parent. Teachers can capitalize on this valuable information from parents to capture the interest of the child in class work and get to know the student on a more personal basis. Also, if the teacher knows about financial, health, or other family tensions the teacher can help the child cope and concentrate on the child's academic progress. (Adapted with permission from the November 1995 issue of *The School Administrator.*)

Enoch concludes that, ". . . The parent-teacher conference is a wonderful opportunity for both the parent and the teacher to gain important information about the child and to build a stronger bond between school and home" (pp. 24–26). Therefore, it is a challenge for you the principal to be sensitive to the parent-teacher conferencing skill level of each teacher and take the necessary steps to provide ongoing staff development for those who need help with this vital skill area.

MULTICULTURAL ISSUES AND PARENTS

Our multicultural, multilingual society presents major barriers to open communications. You as principal must be sensitive to these cultural and language differences and to the reluctance of poor or non-English speaking parents to visit you or their child's teacher. When this language diversity exists, interpreters/translators in the community can prove very helpful to you and the parent. The use of community bilingual volunteers should be a high priority to help you succeed as principal in a language diverse community. Lyn Miller-Lachman and Lorraine S. Taylor (1995) suggest that helpful parent training programs for linguistically- and culturally-diverse parents and extended family members are vital to effective parent-teacher communications. They believe that grandparents and other relatives should be invited to participate in training sessions. Also, Lachman and Taylor believe that, ". . . Religious organizations, social agencies, grass roots community organizations, libraries, and community leaders can help advertise training in community-based, after-school programs and . . . training sessions and methods of sharing information with the family members should reflect the specific needs of parents. Many parents feel more comfortable in sessions that employ an informal and participatory format for information sharing" (pp. 370–371).

What people value, how they see themselves, and how they see others are products of the culture that they have inherited from their families and the social contexts in which they have lived. This cultural identity is most powerfully represented by the language they speak. Linguists have shown beyond question that not only does our experience shape our language, but that our language also structures our experience. Since all language makes use of metaphor, people who use different words to describe a different object or event genuinely see these things differently. Language is personal and inextricably tied up with a person's self image. When a person's language is ridiculed or denigrated, that person him- or herself is attacked.

As a result, people from different cultures or with different languages (or even different dialects of English), are often uncomfortable around groups of "locals" who seem secure and superior in their own language enclave. Many parents from linguistically different or poor backgrounds are intimidated by the professional people in a school who speak in a special language that serves to insulate them from outsiders. (Many middle-class, English-speaking parents are also intimidated by the professional jargon of schools!) Clearly, most educators who engage in this intimidating linguistic behavior are not aware of the negative impact they are having. However, it would probably be a good idea for every school to perform its own "linguistic audit."

This linguistic audit need not be a complicated procedure. A principal might initiate one by asking people associated with the school, from different socioeconomic groups and different language and dialect backgrounds, to give honest feedback on how they feel when they hear the school's professionals speak, when these professionals talk to them, and when the professionals talk to each other. Having laid out this "simple" procedure, it is evident that it is not really that simple to accomplish. How can you get a nonnative speaker of English, a local farmer or automobile worker, or an African-American parent to perform this service for you?

Obviously, not everyone who is a member of a particular group, is willing to do the job or will do it equally well for you. But if you start with the school's obvious stakeholders (most notably parents), you can introduce your appeal with a sincere plea for help. In most cases you won't be turned down. As you, the principal, read this, you are probably already identifying some of the different cultural groups that should be represented in your audit and are thinking of individuals who will be willing to help and will do a good job as auditors.

The success of such a linguistic audit, which we hope you will pursue, will depend directly upon how greatly you value the information which your informants provide you. Remember, the ultimate purpose of your school is to serve the children, and this purpose will be best served when parents and other stakeholders have become your active partners and supporters. This will happen when you most effectively communicate with them; effective communication will happen when language has become a bridge rather than a barrier. Parents and other stakeholders who provide this service for you deserve you deepest gratitude.

Once begun, the linguistic audit can be extended into a full blown multicultural sensitivity audit. Your language "auditors" can probably also provide valuable insights about school practices and customs that are offensive and demeaning to certain groups. The principal and faculty need to pay close attention to what they learn from this audit. Just because an individual or group is offended by something in the school, this does not automatically mean that the offending object or procedure must be eliminated. There may be truly necessary reasons for maintaining it; however, it needs to be given careful attention. Its identification provides an occasion for careful self-examination.

When language patterns or school procedures are clearly creating barriers, they should be examined to see how they can be changed. Sometimes this will be relatively easy, and the school's decisive action in destroying barriers will be a powerful symbol of the school's willingness to meet the needs of all its stakeholders. Other situations will be more difficult and cannot be changed without creating new difficulties. These difficulties need to be presented openly to the multicultural auditors, together with an invitation to them to work with the principal and staff to create a workable solution that is acceptable to everyone concerned.

The audit alone will solve nothing. You and your staff need to be committed to overcoming the cultural and linguistic barriers that have been identified. This is no small order; but keep in mind that a problem well-defined is partially solved. The remainder of the solution will flow from your dedication to the education of all children in your school.

BUILDING PARENT CONFIDENCE IN THE SCHOOL

Successful principals know that public confidence in public schools is waning each year, and to regain community respect and achieve more tax support, parent partnerships must be strengthened. Parents' and others' opinions about the success of your school may vary from yours, but you must be sensitive to how they feel. Each year there are more calls for vouchers, private schools, or charter schools. A recent report by Public Agenda, "Assignment Incomplete: The Unfinished Business of School Reform" (Ann Bradley, *Education Week*, October 18, 1995, pp. 1 & 13), revealed that Americans want public schools to succeed, but their confidence in them is fragile. Among the highlights of the report:

 • Nearly 6 in 10 parents with children in public schools would send them to private schools if they could afford them.

 • Almost half of the respondents did not believe earning a diploma from their local high school guaranteed that a student had mastered the basics.

 • Only about one-fourth of the population can be described as "lovers of learning" who advocate, for example, teaching European and Asian history and classic literature.

 • Eleven percent of teachers picked academics as the most important factor in career success, 50% cited inner drive, and 33% backed knowing how to get along with others.

Most of the experts on school reform believe that it has not lived up to its advanced billing because insensitive school officials have excluded the local people from the reform loop. Administrators and policymakers at the local level talk a big game about parent, community, and business involvement in decisions that really change schools for the better, but go about making token appointments, ignoring their suggestions, and making the decisions themselves. As a result of this neglect of meaningful dialogue and ignoring local advice and counsel, parents and others are out of patience with public school governance procedures. To regain local confidence, damage control must start with parents in new and honest ways.

SCENARIO #6:
DO YOU HAVE GANGS AND DRUGS IN THIS SCHOOL?

A parent who is overly concerned about discipline in the school is a problem waiting to happen. Several times a year a real estate agent will bring a prospective client to a school for a visit. The agent hopes that by visiting the school, the parents will be impressed and decide to buy in that area.

When visiting with the parents, a great deal of sensitivity is essential. Also a high degree of professionalism is necessary. Professionalism impresses the parent by exhibiting competence. Be honest in your evaluation by pointing out the strengths of the school. Weaknesses of the school should also be discussed, and programs which are in place to address them should be presented.

When parents are seeking information, it is important to try to assess the type of situation from which they are coming. Have them describe their current school and then draw similarities to your system. By listening and clarifying situations to which they are accustomed, you can present your programs which are comparable. In doing this, a degree of comfort for the parents can be established.

The Smiths came in on such a visit. They were preoccupied with disciplinary topics. The principal determined they were from a small community which was not, according to them, "plagued" by drugs and gangs. It was important for the principal not to dismiss their fears, because if they did enroll their child and they then perceived that the principal had sugar-coated the situation, major problems might have arisen and the principal's credibility would be diminished. The principal gave them statistics about those issues as they related to the school and community. He explained what programs were in place to secure the safety of their child. In no way did he imply that the community from which they came probably experienced some of the same or similar problems. By not criticizing their perspective, they perceived that a professionalism existed in which they could place their confidence. He then outlined several ways the parents could help protect their child from these influences.

The principal endeavored to portray the community in a positive light. In doing so, he tried to create an atmosphere of trust and concern.

The visit concluded. Later the agent called to express her thanks and complimented the principal on the meeting. She indicated that the parents later revealed that the school from which they were moving did have gangs and drugs and that his candid approach reassured them that he was proactive in his approach to dealing with such problems.

About 2 weeks later the parents enrolled their daughter, and things went well for about 3 weeks. Then one morning a frantic mother called and explained that her daughter had come home with a story about some girls who were passing around some drugs in the P.E. locker room. When the girls realized that they had been seen, they tried to intimidate her daughter. The details were vague but disconcerting nevertheless.

Armed with limited information, the principal immediately began to investigate. The more he probed, the less he found. It was becoming apparent that it was possible that the girl had fabricated the whole incident. How do you tell parents the truth, especially when they had previously indicated a concern about this subject? He called the mother and asked that she come in and visit. He then outlined everything that he had done to investigate the situation. Due to confidentiality issues, the principal revealed only the information and presented a scenario which he thought was probable. He indicated that her daughter probably embellished her story. He explained that this was not uncommon given the circumstances. He stopped short of accusing her daughter of misrepresenting the facts. He then called the girl in and discussed the situation and what he had found. He told her that he appreciated her concern and help. He also assured her that he would do everything possible to protect her. He then explained some things she could do to protect herself.

The mother seemed to be satisfied, but the principal felt that a concern still existed. He assured her that he would closely monitor her daughter in order to protect her. For the next few weeks, the principal visited with the girl and reported to the mother. After 3 weeks all seemed to be going well. The girl had made friends and liked her teachers. By the end of the year, the parents were thanking him for a good year.

Although nothing dramatic was done in dealing with the parents of the girl, the sensitivity expressed for the parent's concern promoted a successful outcome. It shows that often by doing the little things, the big things will work themselves out.

Parents need to be in new and more important conversations about how the schools, teachers, curriculum, and counseling can help their children and youth succeed in a global society that grows more competitive and complex each hour. Parents are worried. Julia Stratton (1995, p. iii) says it this way:

> . . . For the first time in history, a generation of young people is expected to fare worse economically than their parents. We are afraid for them—afraid they'll never the live the American dream. At the same time, we don't always understand them, and that makes it difficult to help them achieve that dream.

Principals who are true "champions for children" will search every possible avenue to build parental involvement into meaningful reform and school improvement plans. Parents are the first and should be the best teachers for their children. Regardless of the economic stature and education level of mothers or fathers, their children are their most precious possession. As principal, your challenge is to discover more and better ways to help them help you produce successful and caring citizens for the 21st century.

SENSITIVITY TO THE NEEDS OF THE COMMUNITY

Much of what we have said about parents applies as well to the community at large. In some communities, you, as principal, are viewed as a hero, and in others you are suspected of incompetent leadership. Observers of communities surrounding schools find that lower income, blue collar communities are less observant and critical of their schools and educational professionals. The reasons for this are varied but focus on respect for education and the status it brings to individuals. While some blue collar communities have people with bad memories from their school days and no desire to go visit a school, they do respect education and encourage their children to perform well and not dropout as they did.

An assistant principal in Midland, Texas, learned how to keep many poor Hispanic kids in school. In conversations with community leaders about poor school attendance patterns among their children, the assistant principal asked for their help. In every conversation, community leaders, and especially the fathers of the kids, talked positively about helping get their kids to school. However, when harvest time came or when the Hispanic family needed help on a job, the kids disappeared for long periods of time. The assistant principal had a real advantage in being known in the community because on Sundays he played first base on the local LULAC baseball team. This Hispanic team welcomed one Anglo since one of the assistant principal's Hispanic friends was the team manager. The administrator and his wife traveled and ate with the team and families and got to know them very well. When the administrator had any trouble with a child, he mentioned it the next Sunday afternoon, and the problem was resolved. The dropouts were few and the support from the Hispanic community grew through the year. The assistant principal learned that year what poverty and community neglect can do to the heart and head of a child. His learning curve was exponential because he had taught and coached in a high school and junior high in upper-income communities, and the only Hispanic kids he had known were those few in his science classes and on his baseball teams. Even the most gifted Hispanic kids had pressures that he knew little about.

While serving as a head baseball coach in an upper income high school in west Texas, he had coached an outstanding Hispanic student athlete. The student was a 3-year starter in basketball and an all district pitcher on the winning baseball team. The coach contacted a university baseball coach about his star and the coach signed the athlete to a 4-year full baseball scholarship. He became an instant star in college baseball, pitching his team to the College World Series in his first season. After the school year, the young man came home and pitched for the LULAC team, got a job with the city on a garbage truck and never returned to the university. When the high school coach found out about this tragic turn of events, he called to find out why this promising young man with a bright future would throw away such an opportunity. The young man's response was that he felt out of place at the university, that his family needed him at home to put food on the table, and that his best friends wanted him to stay in town. That coach still grieves over that one life and the promising career that was changed by community and family pressures.

According to sociologists, "marginal men" are those from one ethnic or racial origin who try to succeed in another culture while keeping their roots in their own culture. They feel that they do not fit in either culture and usually return to their local communities and familiar surroundings. It takes strong and persuasive leadership on the part of a school principal to bring change in community thinking about education and success for children. High visibility in the community at civic clubs, churches, and community gatherings, on the part of the principal and the teachers, can do wonders to build bridges between the school and its community. If community members sense that the principal really cares about the welfare and future of all children and youth and if the principal can plan programs that bring the community into the school, the principal can build a "field of dreams" for kids.

WHEN COMMUNITY INTEREST LEADS
TO COMMUNITY PRESSURE

Middle- and high-income schools have many similarities with low-income schools and also many differences. In these upper-income schools, community members are usually college-educated, successful professionals who offer free advice to school principals about how to manage their schools. These community members come to visit the school, invited or not, and can build strong interest groups to influence everything from cheerleader selections to curriculum decisions. While this intense attention can reap many benefits in the form of equipment, tutors, scholarships, and other advantages for the students, there is often the price of too much interference and meddling with the educational side of the school. Extremist groups from religious and political sectors apply enormous pressures on what is taught and how it is taught in the school. To ignore or insult these groups is tantamount to professional suicide for the principal.

A community attitude survey was conducted in an upper-income community to investigate the opinions of all community sectors about the types of skills and knowledge that their children needed to succeed in the 21st century. The school administration and the survey task force, comprised of community leaders and educators, worked with a university professor to insure that all sectors of the community were given the opportunity to express their opinions—especially the extremist groups. Groups and individuals were purposely invited to open forums to help build the questionnaire that would be mailed to a stratified random sample of the community. Despite the attempts to include all groups, the effort fell short. After completing one open forum in a high school and gathering excellent ideas for the question-naire, the professor's assistant walked out to the parking lot to find flyers from the local Eagle Forum, a conservative national religious organization, on the windows of each car. Even though the school district administration invited all people to the open forum to gain their perceptions, some people found it necessary to express their opinions through flyers on windshields, rather than through attendance at the meeting. Perhaps these individuals felt that the school leaders had not been sensitive to their concerns in other surveys and felt the need for an alternative measure to give their input.

SCENARIO #7: SPECIAL PRESSURE GROUPS

Dealing with special interest groups in the community is a perplexing problem. It is difficult because the group rarely exemplifies the community as a whole, but is a problem in that they are usually quite vocal. The Eagle Forum is a prime example.

A principal's first contact with the Eagle Forum came when he was approached by a parent who, under the Hatch Amendment, made certain demands of the school. Although several different areas were discussed, a major focus was on the area of curriculum. To put it briefly, the parent wanted all of the textbooks and curricular documents used in her child's classes. She indicated that she would then review them and indicate which were suitable and which were not to be used with her child. She was expressly concerned with anything that taught a non-Christian moral or dealt with any form of witches, goblins, or evil. During their initial meeting, the principal restated the parent's concern and told her he would see what could be done to address her request. He told her he would review what needed to be done and would contact her promptly regarding how they could meet both her request and the school's responsibility. The principal knew that rejecting her request would lead to negative publicity, but he didn't want to compromise the District's integrity.

After reviewing the Hatch Act and District policy, he determined that the best course of action was to provide as much information to her as possible. The District did not have a protocol for reviewing curricular materials. He arranged for copies of textbooks, curriculum guides, and ancillary materials to be placed in the Principal's office.

The principal called the parent and scheduled to meet with her. In this meeting, the strategy was to involve her in the decision-making process regarding the materials used in her child's classes. The principal would avoid taking sides and would focus attention on the educational program. In the meeting, the principal and parent first went over her concerns. The principal then presented the school's position in relation to mandates of the state regarding the curriculum. In this meeting, agreement was reached that there was nothing in the state mandates or the local adoption of the curriculum used that was objectionable. However, she was still concerned about specifics in the classroom. The principal suggested that the parent review all of the textbooks and guides and list anything she questioned. From this, they could discuss the matter further. She agreed. All the materials would be in the library for her to review. For several days, she came and stayed for about an hour each day. Finally, after 2 weeks, she asked to see the principal.

This conference was very interesting. She had reviewed only one textbook. She had made scanty notes and was not able to specifically object to any particular story or exercise. As they reviewed her questions, it became clear to the principal that she could not find anything objectionable. She did say that she would like to review more but that she hadn't realized how much time it took. She agreed that the principal had been most accommodating. The principal assured her that anytime she had a question, he would be more than happy to discuss it. He never heard from her again.

Although this could have been a blockbuster, it resolved itself positively. The potential for serious problems existed, but by being open and helpful, this parent was accommodated. Later, the principal found out that this was a test case by a small special interest group. A reporter-friend told him she had been contacted about a story relating to this incident. When the group found they had no story because of the school's cooperation, the request was dropped.

Two lessons should be learned from this. First, there will always be a special interest group looking over your shoulder. Second, a strategy for dealing with them is critical. A good protocol should have in it the following elements:

- ◆ Provide information at all times.
- ◆ Involve the group in decision-making.
- ◆ Avoid taking sides.

- ◆ Focus on larger issues (don't get trapped debating technicalities).
- ◆ Have published procedures.

The last suggestion is important because it's only a matter of time before a parent or group finds something to which they object. The best resource is to have procedures that allow for the review of materials without interfering with day-to-day operations. In this instance, the principal didn't have a procedure. Therefore, it was conceivable that considerable time might be spent responding to the parent's request. Established procedures should detail the due process of registering a complaint. Included in this should be a system that allows individuals to copy materials. This fosters efficiency and is good public relations. The district should have a form that requires all the relevant data describing the complaint. It should also include what has been done to resolve the complaint and a description of the proposed resolution.

In dealing with special interest groups, there is no guarantee of success. All the procedures and cooperation in the world may still lead to confrontation. However, the lack of procedures and cooperation will surely lead to conflict. It's better to be prepared, than to fly by the seat of your pants.

Perhaps the worst thing the principal can do is to assume that the special interest groups that operate in the school's community are out to destroy the school and what it is trying to accomplish. This may be true; but quite often it is not, and the paranoid assumption that the members of these groups are necessarily antagonists will certainly lead to confrontation that will negatively impact the school program. Most individuals who are members of special interest groups, like the Eagle Forum mother described in this scenario, are not guided primarily by negative motives but by a genuine desire to see that a good education is provided for their own children and for other children in the community. The best course to take in responding to them is to open the school so that they can fully see what is happening, and, if possible, make them partners in the school improvement process. This will not always be possible; in many cases what special interest groups demand is demonstrably wrong in terms of good educational practice. At these points the principal needs to take a gentle but firm stand, supported by clear evidence that supports what the school is doing. This approach won't solve all the problems of vocal interest groups, but it will help focus the debate on educational issues, not on secondary matters. It will hold the door open for future cooperation with members of the interest group and for the eventual achievement of a mutually satisfactory solution.

Community feelings run high in schools that place high demands on the principals and teachers. Keen principals can capture this zeal and turn it into opportunities for the students and the staff. By keeping your poise while being told how to run your school and while being told by your PTA and business advisory groups how much they know about teaching, learning, coaching, and managing, you can do wonders for your school. Just bite your lip and use strong emotional intelligence; tell your advisers how much you appreciate their wonderful help, and miracles can happen. After you win your community leaders' attention through good listening skills, ask about ways to acquire better computers for your kids and staff and seek funds for field trips. Also, seek funds for scholarships for your teachers, assistant principal, and you to return for summer graduate classes or to go on planning retreats with the staff.

Long-time observers of school principals have found that good listening and patience pay great dividends around experts who know more about your job than you do. Win over your community by promoting each kid and by inviting people to become involved in helping you and the staff help all children be successful citizens. Kids are the best solution to community-school problems. By focusing on the "Generic Kid" and not on personality or role conflicts, most school issues can be confronted and problems can be resolved through good listening skills, high community visibility, and a moral sense of what is lasting and right for all children. Joyce Epstein (1995, May, p. 701) expresses the power of school/family/community partnerships this way:

> ... There are many reasons for developing school, family, and community partnerships. They can improve school programs and school climate, provide family services

and support, increase parents' skills and leadership, connect families with others in the community, and help teachers with their work. However, the main reason to create such partnerships is to help all youngsters succeed in school and later life. When parents, teachers, students, and others view one another as partners in education, a caring community forms around students and begins its work.

SCENARIO #8: PRIDE IN APPEARANCE

Being sensitive to community concerns is difficult because of the difficulty in accurately assessing community perceptions and needs. It takes a secure and proactive principal to take the risk of looking at the school through the community's eyes. Principals who are insecure in the school system or the community tend to avoid determining community perceptions.

A favorable community perception does not guarantee school effectiveness, but the lack of it will likely insure a lack of sustained improvement. With this in mind, Harry Crenshaw initiated a study using various techniques. Two important ones were a principal's advisory committee and the NASSP Climate Survey. Both were designed to look at community perception.

Having lived in the community all his life, Harry felt he had a good idea of what the community values were and how the community perceived the school. The school where he was principal was located in a "rough" part of town. Built in 1958 it had had only two principals before he became principal in 1984. As an assistant principal at the school, he had developed a significant reputation in the community. All the seventh graders in town came to his school. Over 900 students were in a building built for 500. The school was in a low socioeconomic neighborhood, with a public housing project down the street. That project was so rough that firemen would not enter unless accompanied by a police escort.

From working with the faculty, Crenshaw knew that the education offered was excellent. The teachers worked in a cooperative relationship and had high morale. Achievement test scores were above average. Attendance was high and dropout rates were low. But what about the public? His concern about the community perception began as he heard comments like "Aren't you scared to work there?" or "What kind of problems do you have with the neighborhood?"

Previous to this, the Principal's Advisory Committee had only been discussing academic topics. The first thing on the agenda for the next meeting was community perception. In the meeting, it became obvious that somewhat different perceptions were operative. First, teachers believed that the students were learning and comfortable, but that the public had a negative feeling about the school. Parents agreed that the education of the kids was great and the children themselves felt OK about the school. Their discomfort was not with the school but with the neighborhood.

The problem was how to change public perception. This was not going to be an easy task. No one on the Advisory Committee had a solution. Using the Nominal Group Technique, solutions were generated which might help solve the problem. Projects to implement these solutions were planned.

First, the issue of security of the campus emerged. There were concerns that potential problems existed before and after school and that a more visible form of security would help parents feel better. It was noted that teachers were on duty during these times, but that going to and from school was a problem, especially because of a "hang out" near the school.

Crenshaw approached this in two ways. This was a school problem and a community problem. From the school's point of view, he worked with the maintenance department, faculty, and student council. From maintenance, it was suggested that fencing certain areas of the campus would be beneficial. Fences were proposed for locations that helped the appearance of security without making the school look restrictive or unattractive. Crenshaw worked with the faculty to increase their duty stations and initiate a plan to welcome students as they arrived and wish them well as they left. Very simply, teachers and administrators made a concerted effort to wave and/or speak to parents as they dropped off or picked up their children. The student council was asked to design a plan to make the building more attractive.

To tackle the problem of the surrounding community, Crenshaw enlisted the cooperation of the police department. They had also been having complaints about the "hang out" from the area residents. Also, a city block just in front of the building was vacant and unkempt. The feeling was that if these two problems were solved, the school would be seen in a favorable light. Additionally, it was suggested that patrolmen be more visible during the hours when school children were arriving and leaving. Although a large percentage of students were riding buses, a considerable number of local area children walked or rode bicycles to school. The visibility of the police would help those kids' parents feel better about their sons and daughters coming to and leaving school. Through the health department, the police were able to close down the "hang out." It was later condemned and torn down. The owners of the lots in the block in front of the school were contacted and they agreed to keep the lots mowed. Police were near the school every morning and afternoon.

The students, working through homerooms, agreed to develop and maintain a landscape in front of the school. The PTA also agreed to purchase all the plants necessary. With this commitment, the maintenance department agreed to put in a sprinkler system. The student council then worked with a local landscape architect to develop the plan. This did three things: First, it gave the students a real-life problem to solve. All disciplines had lessons relating to the problem. Mathematics classes focused on measurements, language arts classes wrote specifications, social studies classes worked on surveys, and science classes learned botany. All the departments in the school did something relating to the project. Second, because it was their project, it was easy to form rules necessary for its upkeep. For instance, students would not let each other play near the flower beds. Third, it showed the immediate community a pride in the appearance of the area while making the larger community aware that efforts were being made to address their concerns.

The next year, a comparison of the climate surveys with the previous year's showed a marked improvement in community perception. Teacher morale was also higher. Students did not feel as threatened as before. The comments in the Principal's Advisory Committee were more positive.

Being sensitive to the community was key in solving the identified problem. Then taking a proactive attitude, the problem was addressed successfully. Because this problem was recognized as a never ending one, needing constant attention, continued efforts were employed to build upon success.

SENSITIVITY TO THE BUSINESS-INDUSTRIAL COMMUNITY

A large portion of the money that supports most schools comes from taxes that are paid by the community's businesses and industries. The case for taxing business and industry is based on the belief that these institutions will be the chief beneficiaries of good schools. Good schools draw good workers and their families to the community. Good schools make families want to stay in the community. Good schools should produce graduates who are prepared to take jobs in business and industry and who can make positive contributions to community life.

However, business and industry, like many parents, have begun to question whether their local public schools can really be responsive to their legitimate needs and those of the community. They find that many local high school graduates lack both the academic skills and the work habits to be suitable employees. Much of the business-industrial sector of the community have begun to doubt that their large financial contributions to schools are really justified. These community leaders are frustrated. They would like to help change the situation, but they don't know how, and they often feel as though professional educators have erected barriers to their involvement in schools. The principal must be sensitive to these perceptions and must work systematically to change them.

Most school districts in urban and suburban areas have established some form of school-business partnership. Jerry Barber, Superintendent of the Socorro Independent School District, El Paso, Texas, has reached out to the business community to help the teachers and the students they serve. Since 70% of the

20,000 students in the district are from economically disadvantaged families, Barber needed additional resources to improve the lives of the children and youth in his district. A large percentage of his kids have limited language proficiency and there is a constant flow of immigrants from Mexico. Jerry Barber told the story of the many needs of the children and youth in the community to all who would listen. Community business and government groups listened to his sensitive plea for help and collaborated on a proposal which led to a $15,000,000 Urban Systemic Initiative grant from the National Science Foundation. To receive the grant, local school leaders had to cooperate with municipal governments, school districts, business groups, universities, and other important community groups. With the help of this grant, over 100 businesses established partnerships to help the children succeed in the Socorro schools. Without question, all of the school principals have a valuable resource in these businesses and do not hesitate to call them in for teaching, speaking, tutoring, and computer training for the students, teachers, and parents.

Since the national calls and reports for school reform in the 1980s centered on national economic fears about America's role in international competition, business leaders have become major players in school reform. School principals must be sensitive to those beliefs and work to solve the school problems. Charles and Lynn Meyers (1995, p. 358) identified five key areas in which business leaders have asserted themselves in the business of education:

+ The way in which schools are administered;
+ The push for better teaching of basic skills and vocational education;
+ The adoption of school-to-work plans;
+ Local tax questions; and
+ The teaching of private enterprise ideology.

These five areas are critical to the success of the schools and to the well-being of the students and the community. Principals must be sensitive to the desires of business leaders who want workers who can read instructions, write legible letters, show up at the job on time, and work well in teams. Businesses need intelligent workers and consumers to stay in competition in the global market place. The school-to-work transition can no longer be a hit-or-miss proposition; business leaders are becoming more vocal in their demands on schools. A recent study by Ivan Charner, Bryna Shore Fraser, Susan Hubbard, Anne Rogers, and Richard Horne (1995, September) of 14 existing school-to-work programs across the United States identified 10 key elements that are critical to the success of a school-to-work transition system:

♦ Administrative Leadership

Successful transition systems must have administrators who work with the community to create shared visions, specific goals, and a plan to make things happen for students.

♦ Commitment of Program Deliverers

The school staff must be sensitive to the needs and career choices for students and create flexible career-related curriculum and more relevant teaching strategies to make the world of work and the classroom tightly linked. Students and business leaders must see a close tie to the skills and attitudes needed for success on the job. Teachers who have been teaching in standard classrooms using standard curriculum are so tied to teaching to the state test that they are fearful of changing to a real-world format that may not focus on the essential elements required by the state and the district. When this fear exists among program deliverers, the principal, the superintendent, and the board must give strong support and encourage innovation and change.

♦ Cross-sector Collaboration

All stakeholders must be engaged in the school-to-work program, i.e., businesses, colleges and universities, and community. The change to a transition program requires systemic reform and careful nurturing of each partner.

♦ Fostering Self-determination in All Students

The school-to-work program must be sensitive to the needs of students who range from low achievers to those who are college bound. School-to-work is for all students, who need to know how to think on higher levels and to solve problems presented by an uncertain future. For instance 85% of the technologies needed for a global economy in the year 2005 have yet to be discovered, and 50% of the knowledge taught in 1995 will be obsolete in 5 years. The problem is that futurists do not know which 50% it is!

♦ School-based Learning

Classes need to be designed to connect the world of work with regular classroom instruction. Emphasis on hands-on, real-world learning experiences will not only keep the students' interest but will provide incentives to perform at high levels. This work-classroom connection will help students gain work readiness as well as vital academic skills.

♦ Work-based Learning

Students need a variety of work-based learning experiences that include school-based enterprises, youth apprenticeships, and job opportunities in the community after school and on weekends. The new Career Center in Odessa, Texas, is an excellent example of how a faculty and business community came together to create meaningful work-based learning for the students.

♦ Integration of Career Information

Career guidance and career counseling should begin in the elementary grades to help all students gain a broader vision of future careers and the kinds of work readiness and academic skills required for these careers. Every student should have a career plan that can be updated each year.

♦ Building a Progressive System

Real-world, work-related learnings need to be initiated in the early grades and continue through high school. This approach will teach students about the close link between school and the world of work during their critical formative years and keep them in school. Systemwide coordination of school-to-work programming will help assure a seamless web of career and academic experiences for all students.

♦ Ensure Access to Postsecondary Options

The school-to-work curriculum and the related hands on experiences need to be strong enough to allow a student to enter either the work world or a community college or university. The programs must emphasize life-long learning and be flexible enough to allow a student access to a wide variety of education and training options.

♦ Creative Financing

Money and human resources are basic to a viable school-to-work program. Creative planning and aggressive action is necessary to seek help from federal, state, business, community organizations, and school districts. After a highly visible business-backed effort, a bond issue passed in the Ector County, Texas, school district to create its new state-of-the-art Career Center. Creative business leaders and school administrators combined forces to publicize the need for the Center, and the community responded by passing the bond issue. The business and education communities are beginning to see the benefit of their joint effort in terms of higher student interest in school and the work readiness skills that employers are seeing in the young people on their payrolls.

(Adapted with permission from the September, 1995 issue of the *Kappan*, pp. 40, 58, & 59.)

School-to-work programs are an excellent example and model to bring business and industry into the education of America's children and youth. Many school-business partnerships have done wonders to enhance learning opportunities for students. Philanthropist Eugene Lang's partnership with a Harlem elementary school has produced amazing results in the academic success of its students. Through the "I've Got A Dream Foundation," Lang promised $2,000 toward the college tuition of any student who finished high school. Most of the original 61 students are still in school and expect to graduate (Amundson, 1988, p. 74).

Amundson (p. 80), provides some very helpful questions that school and business leaders need to ask before engaging time and money in a partnership:

+ What are the educational priorities of our district?
+ Who in the community shares a particular interest in helping the district reach specific goals?
+ How can a partnership benefit both parties?
+ What policies and guidelines have we developed for partnerships?
+ How can we turn partnerships into ongoing relationships?
+ What staff are needed to develop and maintain partnerships?

Joyce Dutcher, an elementary science instructional specialist in the Fort Bend, Texas, school district, worked to bring parents and industry together to develop a national partnership model. Strengthened with an idea and a $40,000 grant from Dow Chemical Co., the George Foundation, ALLTEL, Sugar Land Co., Exxon Chemical Co., and the Sugarland Rotary Club, Dutcher worked with the principal and staff of three elementary schools to involve parents in a program called PASP—Parent Assisted Science Program. This hands-on science program for economically disadvantaged students is designed to stimulate greater interest in science through real-life science experimentation and parental assistance. Each school has recruited eager parents to volunteer time and talent to assist teachers and kids with a variety of science projects and activities. The parents are not only helping the schools, they are also gaining job skills. The PASP program is an excellent example of the magic that occurs when school leaders reach out to community organizations and businesses and ask for help for kids (Muck, 1995).

Conclusions

Sensitive principals need to sharpen their sensitivity skills in order to better understand the needs, attitudes, and values of the community they serve. Keeping a sensitive eye on ways to help parents, businesses and community agencies as partners for kids is critical to your success as a school leader. You can be the best instructional leader and teacher motivator in the world, and, yet, if you are insensitive to the needs and opinions of others, you cannot succeed as a principal. Unless you can feel the pain of Armando's father who wants an education for his son, but needs him to help feed his brothers and sisters, you have missed the point about school partnerships and parent involvement. As a result of your sensitivity to others, you should gain support to provide volunteer help in the form of tutors, fund raisers, security assistants, field trip sponsors, and advocates to the school board, the central office administration, and city leaders. The individual friends you make for your school become friends for every child and teacher in your building. Do it for them. Allow your love and sensitivity for the "Generic Kid" to fill your daily thoughts and actions. Your sensitivity to others is the reason that lives will be molded for the good. The following self-assessment instrument (Table 4.1) may help you as principal take stock of your effectiveness in being sensitive to parents, businesses and other community groups and agencies.

TABLE 4.1. PARENT, BUSINESS, AND COMMUNITY AGENCY SENSITIVITY SCALE

Circle the appropriate answer to each question.

1. I have an effective parent contact plan.   Yes   No

2. I visit in the homes of my students on a regular basis.   Yes   No

3. I have a well-designed plan to bring parents into my school.   Yes   No

4. Parents view me as a partner in helping their child.   Yes   No

5. I have instituted a parenting education plan.   Yes   No

6. Parents feel that they can contact me at anytime.   Yes   No

7. I sometimes talk down to low income parents.   Yes   No

8. I am usually a good listener when parents have a concern.   Yes   No

9. Parents trust me to do the right thing with their child.   Yes   No

10. I know the important parents who influence others.   Yes   No

11. I have wide spread contacts with businesses and employers.   Yes   No

12. I have a community advisory group of business/ professionals.   Yes   No

13. I listen well when business leaders express their opinions.   Yes   No

14. I am on a first name basis with key community and business leaders.   Yes   No

15. I have a regular planned system to bring in community resource people to tutor and speak to our staff and students.   Yes   No

16. I trust other children and youth agencies to help my kids succeed.   Yes   No

17. I work hard to assure that individuals of all races and cultures are included in advisory groups and as business partners.   Yes   No

18. I plan regular appearances in business and agency offices.   Yes   No

19. I am willing to ask businesses for money and equipment for students.   Yes   No

20. I view myself as a servant leader in the community.   Yes   No

SKILL BUILDING ACTIVITIES

1. Work with your teachers to develop a parent questionnaire which can be sent home with students, mailed, or used as a telephone interview format. Include the following questions, as well as others that you should add to adapt it to your situation:

   ♦ Do you believe that the school places the student first in our decision-making efforts?

   ♦ Do you believe that we give special treatment to some students and not to others?

   ♦ Does our school make each student feel important and wanted?

   ♦ Do you feel that the teachers and administrators really want you to come to visit the school?

   Distribute the questionnaire and gather the results for staff discussion and action to improve the school's sensitivity toward its constituents.

2. Ask teachers and other staff members in your school to read the story about the gifted Hispanic student athlete who dropped out of college to work for the city as a garbage collector. Ask each teacher and staff member to think of steps that could be taken to prevent another student from doing the same thing.

   ♦ Organize the staff into small groups (5–8) and ask them to use cooperative group processing and provide three strong ideas on strategies to help young people like the student athlete succeed in life.

   ♦ Ask a spokesperson from each group to share the small group's ideas with the entire group.

   ♦ Gather all of the ideas and distribute them to all faculty and staff.

   ♦ Ask the building leadership team to integrate the ideas into the school improvement plan.

3. Assemble a diverse group of parents and community members who represent the various subcultures and linguistic minorities that exist in your school. Ask this group to work with you in conducting a multicultural sensitivity audit, as described in this chapter. Use this audit with your faculty to plan how the school can become a more sensitive environment for people of all cultural and linguistic backgrounds. Arrange for representatives of your faculty to present the plan to your multicultural auditors for their feedback.

4. If your school does not already have a business partner or if you would like to add other partners, identify one or more local business or industrial establishments who you believe could be valuable partners in the operation of your school. Arrange to meet with representatives of these establishments for the purpose of designing a partnership arrangement that would be mutually beneficial to both them and the school.

5

SENSITIVITY WITHIN THE SCHOOL BUREAUCRACY

The beauty of bureaucracy is that it is a rational system. It is not dependent upon personalities; the task of each person in the organization is defined so that it fits in prescribed fashion with the organizational structure and mission of the bureaucracy. Tasks are not based on personality but on rationality. Relationships between people and tasks are carefully prescribed, as demonstrated on the typical organizational chart. Authority flows downward from the top of the organization to subordinate levels, which in turn exercise authority over those at lower levels. Direction flows downward; reporting for accountability goes upward. Most people in bureaucratic organizations want to do the right thing in their positions in the bureaucracy. However, the fact that good people are pursuing rational ends is no guarantee that their combined pursuit will be mutually efficacious or even totally rational. The flaw in bureaucracy is its blindness to the personal and interpersonal elements that permeate every human system.

Organizational systems theorists continue to study the ongoing struggle between the needs of the individual in the school and the rules and policies of the system that bump up against those individual needs. Getzels and Guba (1957) created a formula to explain this dilemma, i.e., $B=f(R \times P)$, or behavior (B) is a function (f) of the interaction between role (R) and personality (P). A person's personal needs and personality are frequently ignored in a bureaucracy bent on reaching a quota or conforming to external directives. Edwards Deming, the late TQM advocate, understood this organizational flaw all too well and frequently chastised managers for blaming the worker for poor production, when in most cases it was the system that was at fault. Individual trust and an open working environment that encourages individual initiative is proving over and over to be the key to organizational efficiency and effectiveness.

Public schools are bureaucracies. As an organization, the school is usually nested within a larger organization—the school district. The school district in turn is a creature of the state and is one level in the bureaucracy of the state educational system. As in any bureaucracy, authority flows downward and accountability flows upward. The heads of units and subunits (state commissioner, district superintendent, principal) are said to have "line authority."

Each head is usually assisted in exercising line authority by a number of staff members (usually expanding at upper levels of the bureaucracy), who are said to have "staff authority." Since these staff members only have authority as they act in the name of the head of their organization, their interpersonal contacts with people at subordinate levels are often marked by uncertainty, often protected by a mask of pseudoprofessionalism. Professionals at lower levels often wonder if these staff members ("coordinators," "consultants," "supervisors," "specialists") are really speaking in the name of their boss or if they are imposing their own will. These staff members in turn are often caught in a difficult situation. They have usually been hired for their expertise in some specialized area, but the real world that they face in the schools seldom exactly fits what their job description has described. They often find themselves trying to convince teachers and principals to follow some path that they feel is right, but often without adequate knowledge of the local campus environment and sometimes unsure if they have the necessary backing from the superintendent. The legitimate influence that they have is based on their expertise; but many are often unsure that either their boss or professionals at subordinate levels will recognize their expertise or its relevance. In this situation of interpersonal uncertainty, bureaucratic structures do not encourage expressions of self-doubt or the search for collaborative solutions.

Because of the basic flaws of bureaucratic structures, principals and their teachers often find themselves in conflict with central office staff. This is a place where the principal's sensitivity skills can facilitate communication and mutual support. The sensitive principal will recognize the difficulties that the supervisor from the central office faces in working with professionals at a school and will also recognize the negative impact that this individual's well-intentioned message can have on a group of hard working but frustrated teachers. There are some central office staff members and teachers who are abrasive or incompetent, but most individuals in both groups are reasonably competent and positively motivated. The problem is usually not in the people, but in the system that dehumanizes them by defining them in terms of a position in the bureaucracy rather than by their personal qualities and ambitions. Sensitivity is essentially recognizing the human elements that exist in a situation and making sure that the situation serves those human needs.

SCENARIO #9:
MAKING THE CENTRAL OFFICE EFFECTIVE

Sometimes one of the most difficult things that a principal must do is to work effectively with central office supervisors, to recognize their personal and professional needs, and to help them be effective in working with the school's faculty. These supervisors occupy an essential place in the educational system, but have very little power. They are sometimes viewed by the faculty as wasted resources. A typical conflict between a supervisor and a faculty is often rooted in the dynamics of organizational change. Teachers, comfortable and secure in their current ways of doing things, don't want to change, while supervisors, whose job descriptions emphasize educational improvement, encourage change. This causes conflict. The principal's dilemma is to support the supervisor while not alienating the staff.

In trying to improve the math curriculum at one middle school, the mathematics supervisor needed to play an essential role in introducing new materials and methodology. Her mandate proceeded from the Assistant Superintendent for Instruction, who was performing in line with his own mandate from the superintendent and board. It was the principal's job to coordinate the integration of this supervisor's expertise and resources with the faculty's task of developing and delivering an improved curriculum.

The mathematics curriculum had not been updated for several years. It was based on a mastery learning model, but its implementation had led to tracking of students by ability. Also, the level and content of the teaching units were inadequate to prepare students for the rigors of high school mathematics.

The supervisor was trying to implement a change in both the curriculum and implementation. The teachers, while admitting problems with the scope of the curriculum, were upset by the suggestion of rethinking the tracking of students. How was the principal going to mediate or convert a turf battle into a meaningful exercise in change?

The principal felt a sensitivity to both positions. On the supervisor's side, the principal agreed with the direction for changing the curriculum. He also was sensitive to the teachers in that the call for change might be interpreted as an indication that they were not doing a good job. His problem was to get the teachers to buy into change and become enthusiastic partners in it. He knew that if their self-esteem were destroyed, no productive change could occur.

The principal's first strategy was to assume that the professionalism on both sides would be sufficient to achieve the desired goals. However, after the initial meetings proved to be nonproductive, the supervisor was upset and the faculty was belligerent. As the principal reviewed what had occurred, he realized that he had failed to lay a proper foundation for the change and that it was time for him to become more personally involved.

Back to square one. Hopefully, the damage was not so devastating that the situation couldn't be reversed. Knowing that the curriculum needed changing, the principal had to find a way to help the teachers recognize the need to change. He also had to support the supervisor as a valuable resource. Where should he begin?

First, he visited with the supervisor, complimenting her efforts and asking her help in planning future strategy. He listened sympathetically while she described how her efforts had been rebuffed by the faculty. Without making any judgment about the attitude or ability of the faculty, the principal offered to work with the faculty to prepare them for the change. They agreed that the supervisor's involvement should be curtailed for the time being.

Next, the principal had to develop a plan to get the faculty to seriously consider the need for change. This was done by having the mathematics faculty explore two areas: (1) the current thinking about math expectations for the grades being taught in the school, and (2) the pros and cons of ability grouping and how it applied to the situation. Teachers were also sent to mathematics teachers' conventions and to schools that had exemplary programs. Responding to the needs and requests of the teachers, the principal created study groups among the faculty for the purpose of analyzing research, school data, and information gained from conventions and school visits.

After a period of study, the principal asked the faculty to make recommendations on the direction needed for the improvement of the mathematics curriculum. They suggested that the curriculum be improved to meet higher standards and more appropriately address the essential knowledge needed for success in higher mathematics. They further recommended that the tracking of students needed to be modified.

The situation was now ready for the supervisor to reenter the process. The principal shared the faculty's decisions with her and asked her what she thought the next steps should be. The supervisor, recognizing now the autonomy that the staff needed, indicated that she was quite ready to take a helpful, supporting role to help them implement their decisions.

Overall, the principal in this case exercised good interpersonal sensitivity in perceiving the needs and concerns of both the supervisor and the faculty and in achieving a highly desirable educational outcome. Revitalizing the mathematics curriculum, largely as originally envisioned by the supervisor and the principal had been accomplished. Equally important, the faculty felt empowered in determining their own destinies and controlling their own curriculum offerings, and the supervisor felt that she had gained stature with the faculty.

It could be argued that if the principal had been more sensitive to the precarious situation of the supervisor in the first place, the process of rewriting the curriculum would have proceeded more smoothly at the beginning. However, what is more important is that once he recognized the interpersonal difficulty of the situation, he demonstrated sensitivity to both supervisor and faculty and was able to successfully intervene. What was demonstrated was that simple verbal support of the supervisor was not enough. Principals will often find that they must take time to help central office staff work with their school faculties and must prepare their faculties for central office assistance.

THE RESTRUCTURING VISE

Currently American schools are facing demands to restructure and reform what they are doing. These calls for restructuring and reform have come from many sources. The costs of education have increased at the same time that the need for additional social services have increased. Changes in the nation's social structure and public expectations have put demands on schools that were not made 25 years ago. As the national conscience has rightly required that all students, including the handicapped and those from diverse backgrounds, be provided educational opportunities equal to those provided to nonhandicapped students from middle class families, the other social institutions (e.g., the family, churches, etc.) that have traditionally supported education have also been negatively impacted by the changing dynamics of American society. Because schools are public organizations, the American people and their elected representatives have responded to social crises by demanding changes in the ways that school operates.

Keeping in mind that schools are bureaucracies, any attempts to change them means that their established normal patterns are also going to have to be changed. When this occurs, any patterns that have been established for resolving the tension between individual and organizational needs are necessarily going to be changed. This highlights the tension between personal needs and bureaucratic requirements and increases the likelihood that individuals in the organization are going to be frustrated and alienated. As the school faces restructuring, the principal's skills of sensitivity will be tested to the extreme.

One of the most pervasive forms of restructuring in American schools has included the various strategies for decentralizing the governance of schools, generally considered as forms of site-based management. However, most legally mandated attempts to institute such restructuring have been politically naive, asking for more critical decisions to be made at the school level while still maintaining the legal authority and accountability of school districts.

Jack Greer (1995) believes that it is the height of naiveté for a superintendent and school board to tell principals and site-based teams to make the decisions that fit the needs in their school. When the nation is screaming for national standards in all academic areas and for all educators, such behavior represents a form of organizational blindness—an insensitivity to the vise of conflicting values in which the school and the principal have been placed. States have established tests for high school graduation, and school quality is determined by the percentage of students who master minimum skills tests. Greer concludes that school reforms that require significant decisions to be made at the building level will probably never be successful. The difficulty rests in allowing individual schools the independence they require to implement innovations such as site-based management, teacher and student empowerment, and so on. The problem is that all of the major players believe in a strong bureaucratic school system (p. 323).

Greer's research revealed that some schools succeeded despite this historic artifact called bureaucratic control. Schools that made the most progress had strong cultures of self-determination where faculty expected to be involved in shared governance activities and innovative programming. Successful schools must have a strong-willed principal who will take calculated risks. The best of all worlds is for the principal to have the support of an innovative, risk-taking superintendent who encourages innovation and unique programming on each campus, and is able to work to keep the entire district moving in the same direction to meet minimum board policy and state and national guidelines. However, the superintendent, central office staff, and school board who also support the "Generic Kid," have pressures operating on them to which you, the principal, must be sensitive.

SCENARIO #10: THE FORGOTTEN STAKEHOLDERS

After 2 years of careful planning involving parents, staff, community, and the school board, the superintendent initiated site-based decision making districtwide. The superintendent was very knowledgeable about the new design and was given carte blanche by the school board to implement the plan. Site-based teams consisting of principals, teachers, parents, business leaders, and other administrators were given training in team building and consensus making skills. Visitors came from far and wide to see this well-publicized plan. Several journal articles and book chapters extolled the virtues of this innovative plan to empower each school to make key decisions about personnel, curriculum, and budget allocations. The acclaim and early success of the program gave every indication that this district had done site-based decision-making the right way. However, all of the bases apparently had not been touched and, in the case of one school, the process resulted in disaster.

A new principal was hired to implement the site-based plan in an old traditional high school. The school had gradually changed from an all white, high-performing school to one that had become racially mixed, with lower test scores and a smaller percentage of college-bound graduates. The new principal, the site-based team, and the entire staff moved to implement what they believed to be the best approach to improved student learning—mastery learning, outcome-based programs, and heterogeneous grouping. They changed ninth grade Mathematics and English to mixed-ability classes and eliminated honors sections in the two subjects.

Armed with research on cooperative learning, mastery teaching, and effective schools, and coupled with a strong belief that all students can learn well, that they can help each other learn more, and that they can become more sensitive to other races and cultures, the school staff began the school year.

The word of these changes fell on the ears of affluent, college-educated parents who then complained to the principal that these new changes to mixed-ability classes were "dumbing down" the teaching and learning for their kids. They claimed that the teachers were spending too much time reteaching "those other kids" and therefore their kids were losing their competitive edge for.college and scholarships. However, confident in the supporting research and the virtue of her efforts, the principal politely explained the school's position and indicated that the innovation would be continued. These vocal, influential parents were a force to reckon with. They took their complaints to the superintendent and the board, and the school board listened.

These parents demanded that the honors classes be reinstated and that classes be rigorous for the college bound. The school board yielded to the parents' demands and pressured the superintendent to force the principal and her staff to undo their new mastery, outcome-based plan, and regroup the students. The press picked up the controversy and the new principal was caught in a wedge between her staff and their wishes to continue with their new program and the superintendent, the board, and the adamant parents. The principal was dismayed at the turn of events and defended her position to the press and the parents. She explained the research evidence behind her new plan, but the opposing parents were not impressed. In spite of the superintendent's defending the principal and her site-based team, the board voted to ask the superintendent to tell the principal to reinstate the honors classes and return to the traditional way of grouping students and teaching classes for the college bound. The board accepted the notion that teaching rigorous content the same way to all students would not only prepare students for the finest universities, but would also educate the others to be better in the workforce.

Homogeneous grouping replaced the mixed classes and the ripples of the top-down decisions reached the shores of all of the other schools and site-based teams. They asked: "Do we redo our site-based plan, or do we move ahead with the confidence that the superintendent and board really believed in empowerment and local school site autonomy? What authority do we really have?" (Hoyle, 1994, January, pp. 22–23).

What happened to cause this failure? At least part of it resulted from a lack of sensitivity on the part of both the principal and the superintendent. Since this is a book written primarily for principals, we will examine what she, the principal, might have done differently in this scenario.

The principal had been hired by the superintendent to make site-based decision-making work. Apparently, the principal assumed that she had been given free rein to build her site-based model for the high school. She led her staff to create a curriculum, particularly Mathematics and English, in the ninth grade. The change from traditional honors section to mastery-taught, mixed-ability classes made good sense to the principal and the site-based team, since it was based on research and an assumption of best educational practice. Additionally, the site-based team reasoned that they had been empowered to change their school for the better, and they believed that they knew what was best for the students.

When the parents heard about the changes in Mathematics and English, including the removal of honors classes, they went to the principal for an explanation. She told them that the changes were best for the students, the school, and the community. Also, she told them that the changes were based on sound educational theory and research, and she and the faculty had the backing of the superintendent and the school board. Sensing an inflexible, insensitive attitude on the part of the principal, the parents appealed to the superintendent and the school board to reverse the principal's decision on the Mathematics and English programs and the mixed-ability classes. The superintendent and the board yielded to the parent requests, and the principal was directed by the superintendent and the curriculum director to reinstate the honors programs and eliminate the mixed-ability classes.

The principal was visibly upset by this turn of events and believed that she had been betrayed by the "powers that be," and that site-based decision-making in the school district was in name only. She became so upset that her relationship with the superintendent and the district curriculum director completely soured. Soon after, she left her principal's position.

It would be overly simplistic to assume that greater sensitivity on the part of the principal would have produced a success story in this case. As already noted, the problem was not only the principal's. However, the disaster that resulted was probably avoidable. To build a school that was responsive to its various stakeholders, this talented principal should have engaged many community members and parents in true dialogue before any major curriculum changes were made. Had she been sensitive to parent needs and concerns, much of her grief might have been avoided, and the final result might have been more educationally productive.

Having helped create a problem for the superintendent and school board, the principal seemed unable to recognize that she had in fact reduced their options. Had all parents been invited from the beginning to join the staff as partners to consider the mission of the school as the foundation for curriculum change, they might not have felt isolated from the school, but might have been willing to work with the principal and staff, rather than taking this problem directly to the superintendent and school board. The principal's lack of sensitivity produced problems not only for herself and the school but also for the superintendent and board.

Sensitivity means that you have a deep concern about the feelings of others and are willing to try to incorporate their concerns in a negotiated resolution of the problem. The old "my way or the highway" mentality is inappropriate for emotionally-charged issues surrounding public education of children and youth. Listen with an open mind and heart to others and try to really understand a perspective that may differ from yours. Acts of interpersonal sensitivity will help more students in the long haul, and help you, the principal, balance your loyalties to teachers, parents, children, and superiors.

Among numerous successful efforts by superintendents to transform central offices to be equals and collaborators with teachers and principals in site-based programs is one found in Vancouver, Washington. James F. Parsley (1990), the superintendent, has led the charge to make site-based decision-making more than lip service. In 1990, Parsley and his entire central office staff and representatives from each campus created a new organizational design for school operations. Among the major changes to make site-based decision-making successful was the creation of a new voice for the teaching staff. A districtwide faculty advisory committee issued the following written challenge to help the district move to a new way of running schools:

> Sensing a growing frustration among our colleagues with the status quo, we wish to encourage the school board and the administration to approach their mission with boldness and resolution, to be visionaries rather than fixers, and to seize with enthusiasm and courage this unique opportunity to effect profound and substantive change in the way in which we educate our youth (p. 9).

With this challenge and a lot of careful planning and staff training, the district was transformed. Several central office administrative positions were eliminated, and other positions were revamped to be team workers with each campus improvement team. These changes in the organization were an effort on the part of Parsley, the reassigned central office staff members, and the board to be sensitive to the needs of the children and youth they serve. This flattened organizational structure has eliminated much of the bureaucratic red tape that teachers and principals had to endure for many years under a central office control model. Resource coordinators are assisting and supporting site-based initiatives and professional development activities that are planned and carried out with team leadership in mind. Monthly leadership team meetings for the entire district with teacher representatives are proving to be the key to demonstrating that schools can be autonomous in terms of determining what kids need and how teachers create the best learning environment for the children and youth that attend each school in Vancouver, Washington (p. 14). When changes of this magnitude are underway, you as principal need to be very sensitive to the feelings of the students, teachers, and central office administration.

Another successful effort to develop a districtwide site-based model was begun by Robert Caster, superintendent of the Palestine, Texas, schools. In 1989, Caster saw the need for a new organizational structure to help improve the performance of many of the at-risk students in the schools. Before the state education agency "mandated" site-based decision-making in 1990, Caster and his staff had a plan in place which became a model for others who jumped to the state mandate. The Palestine school board gave total support to the superintendent and his staff to "do it right the first time," and their faith paid off in improved student performance and teacher morale. With the technical assistance provided by a university professor who trained central office and each school's staff in consensus and team-building, the program began with minimum of difficulty. The intense training during the first year included a districtwide team which worked to determine the proper role of each school and of the central office in making decisions. It was determined that the central office staff's role was threefold: first, support for the site-based teams and responsibility for the district's curriculum oversight; second, personnel screening to assure that applicants had the proper credentials and backgrounds; and third, assuring that the budget was balanced after each school received its request. This oversight was not viewed as a "big boss" control but as a conceptual view of how well the entire district was placing personnel and resources where they were needed to help each school reach its goals.

A principal who has a superintendent and central office staff who have not fully grasped the meaning of site-based management and school decision-making is likely to be in for a lot of stress. The stress comes from being caught between a set of explicit expectations and promises of support that are rendered meaningless by bureaucratic regularities that attempt to perpetuate a top-down control system. The support provided in such a contradictory school environment is usually an iron fist in a velvet glove. People smile and speak of shared decision-making, but the realities of conformity persist. The principal must remember that such a situation is generally not the result of evil or incompetent people in positions of power but of well-intentioned people who have not learned how to escape from the predictability and sterility of a bureaucratic system. The principal's sensitivity to the personal needs that are ignored in such a situation will help him or her build and maintain an effective school even under negative circumstances. Persistence may help change those circumstances.

CONCLUSION

It is not easy to be sensitive to and respond accordingly when you have been told that your school will be given the freedom to explore different strategies to make your school more effective, and then have your decisions reversed for various reasons by the superintendent. Systemic change is a slow and painful process, and schools are not generally encouraged to change according to their own needs and at their own pace. School bureaucracies have a tight hold which does not encourage individualism or rogue behavior. In spite of these barriers, you can use interpersonal sensitivity and do the right things for your school.

People who feel controlled by the rules and by a system unresponsive to human initiative will perform only well enough to keep from being fired. When the walls of rules and procedures are created by management, the individual curls up and merely survives. Again the poet Robert Frost reminds us that, "Something there is that doesn't love a wall, that wants it down." However, bureaucracies have grown fond of the walls that keep the power in and try to manage quality from a safe distance. Schools are "loosely coupled," often unpredictable, places where kids act out and teachers struggle to teach under the most difficult conditions. Parents are demanding that each of their children be given special attention, and central offices are demanding reports on time and obedience by the principal and staff. You, the principal, are caught trying to spin 50 plates at the same time and are asked to respond immediately to a request from the superintendent or their assistant. You are being asked to drop all of the plates and run to the central office for a meeting. It takes all of the sensitivity one can muster under these trying and hectic times. A story may help you continue the struggle to do the best in your difficult situation.

An older woman named Hazel tells of a time in her life that has given her strength in times of trouble. She recalls her childhood on a small East Texas farm where she was "raised" along with several brothers and sisters by her mother. The land was poor and what few crops they raised were the family food supply for the entire year. One spring, the crops were in their critical growth stage when a dark cloud developed over their farm and a strong wind followed. Hazel's mother looked up at the clouds and fearing hail which would devastate their crops yelled for the kids to run to the cellar located under the house. Golf ball-sized hail pounded on the tin roof of the old farm house and on the new spring crops. When the storm passed, Hazel recalled that her mother led the kids out of the dark cellar to find utter devastation. The crops were leveled and their livelihood was gone. Hazel's mom dropped to her knees and tears ran down her cheeks as she viewed the destruction. She then said, "Well, children, there is nothing we can do now; let's gather some hailstones and make some ice cream." Hazel recalls with tears in her eyes the strength of her mother when faced with a bleak future for her family. Years later her mother's words still ring in her ears when life's troubles come. When it hails, she still remembers to "gather some hailstones and make some ice cream" (Weld, 1987).

If you, as school principal, can be sensitive to the feelings and needs of others and explore what can be done within the political confines of the system and within the school to help children and youth succeed, then you will make plenty of ice cream.

SKILL BUILDING ACTIVITIES

Look over the sensitivity scale below. Then do the activities that follow.

The Principal's Sensitivity Scale
' Toward the Central Office

Statement	Yes	No	Sometimes
1. I am sensitive to the restrictions placed on the superintendent by the school board.			
2. I am sensitive to members of the central office staff who think they are my boss on all matters impacting our school.			
3. I am sensitive to collective judgment about which decisions need to be made at the central office and which ones need to be made at the school site.			
4. I am sensitive to teachers in my building who are told to follow central office mandates on teaching certain material.			
5. I am sensitive to the reasons that teacher applicants must first be screened by the personnel department in the central office.			
6. I am sensitive to the fact that our site-based program budget was cut in favor of another school which made a stronger case for funds.			
7. I am sensitive that with site-based decision making comes greater accountability demands from the central office.			
8. I am sensitive to the problems I can cause by going off on a tangent that runs counter to district norms and policies.			
9. I am sensitive to pressures that parents place on the superintendent and board to change a program that our site-based team implemented.			
10. I am sensitive to the needs of the teachers and staff in my building and am willing to push central office staff on their behalf.			

1. Use the sensitivity scale above to assess your own sensitivity to personnel in the central office.

2. Ask several people from the central office to use the scale to give their assessment of your sensitivity skills.

3. Use the results of the two assessments to consider how you may improve your sensitivity skills.

6

BUILDING INTERPERSONAL SENSITIVITY

Thus far in the book we have considered the nature of interpersonal sensitivity, the critical significance of a principal's sensitivity to children, and the importance of sensitivity to other adults, whether they be teachers, parents, community members, or central office employees. In this chapter, we consider what a principal must do to build sensitivity, both personally and organizationally.

In their chapter on interpersonal sensitivity in *Principals for Our Changing Schools: The Knowledge and Skill Base* (Thomson, 1993), Muse, et al., identified the knowledge and skill required for a principal to be known as a sensitive leader. First, they focused on what the principal needs to do to receive pertinent interpersonal information. The principal should be able to:

- ♦ Listen carefully and empathetically;
- ♦ Delay the formation of impressions about others until adequate information or observations are acquired;
- ♦ Gain impressions from first-hand knowledge and not merely from the comments of others;
- ♦ Understand the critical importance of maintaining and enhancing the self-esteem of others;

♦ Recognize the individual differences that make people unique;

♦ Learn to differentiate among members of the same group;

♦ Recognize the ways in which others are similar and dissimilar to themselves;

♦ Observe the reactions of others, including nonverbal cues, to better understand situations;

♦ Maintain emotional control;

♦ Recognize that others can grow and that judging habits must allow that growth to occur;

♦ Dismiss inappropriately perceived attitudes, values, and behaviors of others; and

♦ Avoid stereotypes of sex, race or ethnicity.

(Muse, et al., 1993, p. 15-14.)

Second, they looked at how a principal should behave in order to create a caring (interpersonally sensitive) environment. The principal should be able to:

♦ Anticipate the emotional effects decisions and actions might have on others;

♦ Respond tactfully and respectfully in emotional situations;

♦ Elicit the perceptions, feelings, and concerns of others;

♦ Encourage others to share information that is relevant to organizational goals;

♦ Encourage feedback from school groups and respond immediately to their suggestions and recommendations;

♦ Recognize that conflict is inevitable and use it to strengthen relationships;

♦ Follow through on commitments and keep one's word;

♦ Use the name of the other person when conversing with him or her;

- Recognize and praise others;
- Show respect and courtesy toward others;
- Question, clarify, and correct others in a positive and professional manner;
- Suggest compromises;
- Be active listeners by focusing on what is said and by paraphrasing the speaker's views, feelings, and concerns;
- Support others without assuming responsibility for their performance;
- Request assistance to resolve problems; and
- Help others save face when taking a different position.

(Muse, et al., 1993, p. 15-15.)

These are the same abilities that we have focused on throughout this book, and we have provided examples and suggested activities and have provided self-assessment tools to guide the principal toward greater interpersonal sensitivity. But while interpersonal sensitivity may be assessed by checklists, it's not typically built in that way. Something must happen inside the principal. As we suggested in Chapter 1, while sensitivity may be addressed externally, it results from what happens internally. Principals may watch their behavior and words carefully and may say all the right things to avoid offense, but unless there is a genuine caring for the people with whom the principal works and lives, the "correct" actions will only carry him or her so far. In times of social crisis, or over the long-haul, nothing can substitute for sensitivity that starts inside the principal.

Perhaps the first question principals need to ask themselves is: "Do I really value the people around me?" "All of them?" It's easy to value the people who agree with us or who do useful things for us. It's more difficult to value those who think or act differently from us. It's hardest to love the unlovely—particularly if those children or adults seem to be making no contribution at all to the common good. But these are probably the people that need our kindness and sensitivity more than anyone else.

LEARNING ABOUT OTHER PEOPLE AND OURSELVES

Valuing people means understanding them on their own terms. To do this we must listen carefully to what people are saying, not only to their words but also to the feelings that underlie them This is not an easy thing to do, and, as with any worthwhile and difficult skill, it must be developed with practice. We must learn to put ourselves in the place of others we would understand. We must learn to listen.

Look over again the first list of skills, identified by Muse, et al., that a principal must develop to truly perceive and understand other people. In that list, notice the number of times that certain verbs appear and reappear: "listen," "understand," "learn," "recognize," "observe," etc. Notice, particularly, the verb, "delay," that is used in the second skill: *Delay the formation of impressions about others until adequate information or observations are acquired.* These verbs emphasize the depth of this first set of requirements for interpersonal sensitivity and also suggest the direction we may follow to attain it.

Years ago, Joseph Luft (1969) developed a model that he referred to as the Johari Window (Fig. 6.1). The four quadrants of the model represent what people know about each other and what they can learn from each other about the other person and about themselves. The first quadrant is called the "open" quadrant, representing behavior, feelings, and motivations that are known both to oneself and to other people. The second quadrant is the "blind" quadrant, representing behavior, feelings, and motivations that are unknown to oneself but that other persons can recognize. The third quadrant is the "hidden" quadrant, representing the behavior, feelings, and motivations that are known to oneself but not to others. The final quadrant refers to what is "unknown," both to oneself and to others.

The respective size of the quadrants is, of course, unique for any two people. The larger Quadrant #1 is the more that each party knows about the other and the more open the communication between them. Obviously, as Quadrant #1 expands, there is less unknown about one's own behavior and its impact, and the other quadrants must decrease in size. The goal of productive human interaction is to expand what people know about each

FIGURE 6.1. THE JOHARI WINDOW

(Reprinted by permission from Joseph Luft, *Group Processes: An Introduction to Group Dynamics*, Mayfield Publishing Co., 1984, p.60.)

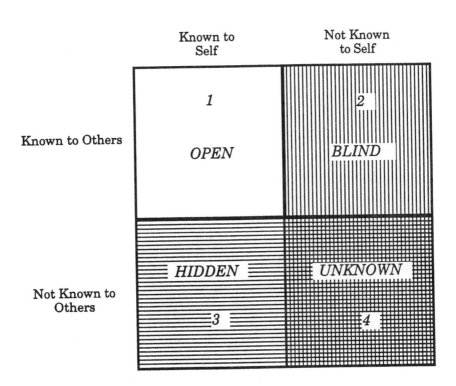

other and about themselves so that they can truly understand the other person and so that they can sensitively adjust their own behavior in response to this enhanced understanding.

What the Johari Window does is to emphasize how much we can learn by listening to other people, not only about those people but about ourselves as well. This tool demonstrates how we can build the base for an open, productive interpersonal relationship by reciprocally providing other persons with what we know about ourselves and what we have observed about them. Such mutual understanding is the basis for an expanded interpersonal sensitivity.

BUILDING THE BEHAVIORS OF
INTERPERSONAL SENSITIVITY

Genuinely listening to other people and understanding them is the foundation upon which any meaningful relationship with them must be based. Once we have developed a relationship with other people that enables us to learn how our words and actions are interpreted by them, we are in a position to learn from them specifically what we need to do to demonstrate interpersonal sensitivity.

We turn now to a consideration of the second list provided by Muse and his associates, the skills that we need to promote a caring environment and what it takes to build those skills into our regular behavior. Turn back to that list now and briefly review it before we continue our exploration.

You may be asking several questions at this point: "Of what value is it to develop a close, open relationship with someone else in order to find out what I need to do to demonstrate sensitivity?" "Can't I simply study the list on my own and incorporate those skills into my regular behavior?" "With how many do I need to develop such a relationship?" "Even one such relationship will take a lot of time; but shouldn't I be learning from many different people from many different backgrounds?"

These are legitimate questions that deserve straightforward answers. Let's begin at the beginning. Yes, theoretically, you *can* learn by yourself to integrate these skills into your normal behavior, but if you are actually able to do it to a significant degree, you are an unusual person. You must remember that it is the person that receives or observes a behavior who is the ultimate judge of its sensitivity, not the person who initiates it. In this arena, self-deception is so easy. Consider nearly any item on that list of behaviors: "anticipate the emotional effects;" "encourage feedback; "encourage others to share information." I may believe that I am doing these things, but if I simply base that belief on my own intentions and perceptions, I can be easily deceived about the actual emotional impact of what I have said or done. Since I can't get inside the thoughts and feelings of others, I can't really know how they have been affected by my words and actions. I may have honestly intended to encourage feedback, but if something unseen by me inhibited the other person, have I really accomplished what I intended? Have I genuinely demonstrated the skill? Probably not.

As to the questions regarding how many people one needs to build such open interpersonal relationships with, we must agree that one person is not enough. On the other hand, it takes time to build a significant open relationship, and our resources of time and energy and our capacity for assimilating the data that will flow from them are limited. There is no simple answer to this, but building one strong open relationship with one person whose views on many things are very different from ours, will be infinitely better than building no such relationship at all. There is much that each of us can learn from the open, perceptive feedback of one other person who has learned to value and care for us just as we have learned to value and care for that person. So, to get started we encourage you to identify one reasonably perceptive person *whom you know disagrees with you on some major issues that involve your work together.* As you get comfortable working with this one person, you may wish to develop similar relationships with others. Always look for perceptiveness and diversity in initiating these relationships. The only thing you must have in common is the belief that you need to learn more about yourselves and your behavior and that this goal can be developed by an open and honest interpersonal relationship.

In the late 1960s, a young teacher, with recent experience as a military officer, was asked to be the assistant principal in a junior high school. Since his first year as a teacher he had been encouraged by administrators and fellow teachers alike to aim his career at the principalship, primarily because his colleagues saw that he was able to take charge of and control a situation and was not afraid to make decisions. Now he was given his first administrative position in a school.

His first impression was that his new job was the most difficult one he had ever had. What made the job difficult was not the amount of paperwork or the large number of legitimate demands from the principal, teachers, students, parents, and the central office, but the fragmented, hostile interpersonal environment that permeated the school. This was a period of student strikes and protests, racial conflict, and the beginning of militant collective bargaining in the district. Being the person who often had to make the unpopular decisions, he was fully aware of the need for understanding the individuals and groups around him and understanding how his decisions impacted them. He felt woefully inadequate. As a military officer, he simply had to make the right decision. Now he had to figure out what a "right" decision was? And who was it "right" for? He knew that what he was doing was inadequate and that he had to learn how to productively interact with other people.

The president of the district's teachers union was a teacher in the same building, and their official roles brought them into frequent situations dominated by tension. They were also different in other ways. It was the time of protests against the Viet Nam war, and their different backgrounds and experiences appeared to put them on opposite sides on that issue. In fact, it seemed as though there were very few points of common agreement between them. However, they each had a genuine and open interest in the welfare of all the children in the building, and they respected each other enough to believe that they could learn from each other.

They decided that they might start by meeting together at a local coffee shop every Thursday morning at 6:00 A.M. before coming to school. The ground rules were simple: (1) no subject was out of bounds; (2) without revealing any confidences, they would let each other know how their words and actions were being perceived by themselves and by others and how effective their behaviors were; and (3) everything they shared was considered as confidential unless they jointly agreed to share it with others.

The impact was quick and powerful. Both partners in the enterprise learned more about themselves and how they were perceived by others. This trial relationship among persons who perceived themselves to be quite different led to the unexpected discovery that there were really many areas of mutual agreement and led to a valued lifelong friendship for each of them. Each learned what was working and wasn't working in his relations with others so that he could adjust his behavior. Further, the impact was felt well beyond their own relationship. Since each was respected among different groups in the school, the school district, and the community, their emerging friendship earned them confidence among members of groups that had been previously closed to them. The assistant principal found that some of his most vocal adversaries now began to seek his wisdom and respect his opinion. Once these initial barriers were broken, he was careful not to do or say anything that would jeopardize their newly developed trust. At the same time, he found that although he still had to take actions that angered some of the school's constituents, the anger was not directed at him personally and he was still able to work productively with these groups to address the school's problems.

Above all, however, the greatest learning for the assistant principal were the insights that he gained about his own behavior and the effect that behavior had on other persons. He also learned to more accurately gauge his impact on others. These were skills, though never again tested to the same degree, served him well in many different positions throughout his career in education. Nearly 30 years later, he testifies that those Thursday morning sessions at the coffee shop were the most valuable professional development seminars he ever attended.

BUILDING RELATIONSHIPS THAT FOSTER SENSITIVITY

What does it take to form the kind of relationship, such as the one just described, that leads to such wide growth and understanding? What enables us to form a productive relationship with people who look at the world from very different points of view from our own? George C. Homans (1950) presented a theory based on the relationship between activity, interaction, and sentiment. Simply put, his theory might be diagrammed as follows:

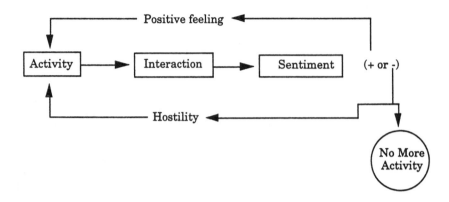

When people come together in an *activity*, they normally engage in a certain amount of human *interaction*. This activity can result in either positive or negative *sentiment*. which is defined as feelings, attitudes, and other human affective states. That is, they can find the interaction rewarding or unpleasant. Whether positive or negative sentiment is produced has powerful implications for what happens next. If the parties have a choice in the matter, they are likely, if their initial interaction produces negative sentiment, to choose not to participate in further common activities. On the other hand, if the activity produces positive sentiment, they are likely to seek further joint activities.

For instance, suppose that a young man and a young woman, who have recently met, decide to go to a movie together. The movie turns out to be a sensational police movie, filled with plenty of violence, high speed car chases, and blood. The young man revels in this and makes no secret about it to the young woman. However, it isn't what she expected, and she is sickened by the movie. Furthermore, she bluntly tells the young man so. Their disagreement leads to some sharp words and some very negative feelings on the part of both the man and the woman. It is very likely that this will be the last time they go out together.

In a school, much activity and human interaction take place, and it results in considerable positive or negative sentiment. However, unlike the example we presented of the man and woman whose joint activity is voluntary on both their parts, most of the people in the school and its environment (principal, teachers, students, parents) cannot easily leave the setting. This means, of course, that human activity and interaction will continue for better or worse. If initial interaction between people in the school (principal-teacher, teacher-student, principal-parent) has resulted in negative sentiment, it is very likely that future activities will produce additional hostility (negative sentiment), unless something is done to break the cycle. Very often it becomes the job of principals to break the cycle, even if they are not directly involved. Why do they often need to become involved in breaking the negative cycle if they are not directly involved? The principal becomes involved because the effectiveness of the school depends upon an interpersonal climate in which individuals feel valuable and supported by their colleagues.

Sensitive principals look for the opportunity to create activities that will bring them into win-win situations with people in the school as well as key individuals in the school's environment (community members, central office administrators, etc.), so that positive sentiment may be built up. This, however, is not enough. The sensitive principal, fully aware that the quality of the school, as a human organization, can be no better than the human interactions within it, looks for opportunities to bring the diverse human elements of the school (students, teachers, parents, classified staff) into activities that are likely to produce positive interactions and positive sentiment.

BUILDING STAFF SENSITIVITY

In large schools it is particularly critical that assistant principals and other key staff display the listening-learning and the speaking-acting behaviors associated with interpersonal sensitivity. Often it is an assistant principal who speaks for the principal and the entire school in emotionally charged and difficult interpersonal situations. Two brief examples illustrate this point.

After the last bell, a middle-aged, harried teacher came to the office of the assistant principal, dragging a big overaged seventh grader behind her. She screamed, "I demand that you whip this boy right now, and I want to watch you do it!" The assistant principal asked, "What did he do?" "He called my best student, who is African-American, a chocolate face, and I demand that he be punished right now!" The administrator in a calm voice said, "Miss Davis, I really appreciate your attention to this serious matter and the concern you have for the little girl who was hurt by the insensitive remark made by Billy. Now let me buy you a coke and let's talk a moment while Billy sits here in my office." After a few sips of the cold drink, the teacher began to regain her composure. The assistant principal said, "Miss Davis, I needed to talk with you about this kid in private for several reasons. First, I am not excusing him for the racist remark, and I agree that you have done the right thing in bringing the incident to my attention. Second, this boy is from an abusive itinerant oil field worker family, and he has an IQ of 89. Third, he is subject to epileptic seizures when under stress and three licks with a paddle would do it. Fourth, paddling this big kid is a futile exercise. He has been beaten more times than we can count by a drunken father. Now, if you will go on home, I will see you first thing in the morning and report my thoughts about how to help this kid and either remove him from your class or assign him to an alternative program."

The next day the teacher came in very early and said, "I wish to apologize to you for my attitude yesterday, and I thank you for the sensitive way you treated me in my state of anger. I should have made the effort to find out more about Billy before yesterday and I will abide by whatever decision you think will work. If you think counseling will help, I will take him back and try and work with him. He really has a sweet nature, but he has no social skills whatsoever, and he has no idea of how his words affect those around him. Again, thank you for keeping your wits when mine were gone."

Another example of an assistant principal standing in the gap in a difficult interpersonal situation occurred in a large high school when an irate mother was called to the assistant principal's office for a conference about a minor rule infraction committed by the mother's tenth-grade daughter. The mother marched into the room and, without acknowledging the assistant principal, began yelling at her daughter about not being able to follow the rules of the school and embarrassing the family name. Before Dee, the assistant principal, could calm the angry mother, the daughter began to cry and look away from her mother's barrage of reprimand. Dee waited until the mother calmed down a little and told her that she and the daughter had already discussed the matter and appropriate measures had been taken to assure that the mistake in behavior would not occur again. The mother appeared to be irritated with Dee's solution and stood up to leave. Dee noticed the big words printed on the mother's T-shirt: "YOU WRITE THE RULES—I BREAK THE RULES." Dee thanked the mother and accompanied her out of the office. After the mother left, Dee comforted the daughter and told her, "Please come and see me if you need to talk." A sensitive school leader kept her cool and helped the daughter through a difficult situation.

What we have said about assistant principals applies equally to all other members of the school's staff: both the professional staff and the classified staff. Every teacher needs these skills in working with students, parents, and colleagues. The school business is a tough one, often filled with tensions that result simply from people carrying out their own roles in the school in the best way they know how. The problem is that often "the best they know how" is derived from the narrow limits of what they perceive to be the objectives of their own jobs. Seldom do they look at others as partners in the enterprise who also have legitimate needs and objectives that may bring them into conflict with their own. When their separate objectives do conflict, they usually view the situation from their own vantage point. They, like the principal, need to learn to understand the people around them and to recognize and support the needs of others. The missions of schools are often damaged severely by teachers, counselors, custodians, or secretaries who are, from their own points of view, simply trying to fulfill the requirements of their own jobs, but without regard for how their efforts impact other people.

Part of the job of the principal is to realize that this is an area where he or she must be a servant, carefully helping professional and classified staff to better understand the people around them and helping them learn how they can positively impact the interpersonal climate of the school. Much of this, of course, will begin with the personal example that the principal demonstrates.

THE PRINCIPAL AS SERVANT-LEADER

The principal succeeds by making everyone else in the school succeed. For the principal there are really no individual rewards. We have spoken regularly throughout the book on how sensitivity must come from within the principal; it cannot be merely adherence to a checklist of supposedly sensitive behaviors. A principal's sensitivity begins with the way that one sees that role in the school. The principal who genuinely has a servant attitude and truly rejoices in the successes of everyone else in the school, whether or not he or she gets any of the credit, has already gone a long way to establishing a pattern of sensitivity in dealing with others.

The sensitive principal knows that the people in the school need resources to do their jobs. Some of these resources require materials and supplies that often stretch beyond the school's budget. Principals need to be the primary advocates for getting the necessary funds from the school district or from private sources, often putting their own reputations on the line and calling in past favors in order to see that students, teachers, counselors, secretaries, cafeteria workers, and custodians get what they need. Principals must, indeed, be sensitive people, but this in no way means that they should be timid persons when a real need exists in the school. Principals should celebrate all the people in the school and do whatever they can to make them succeed.

Of all the resources that teachers and other professional staff members need, perhaps the most important one is time. Unfortunately, the time problem cannot be solved by passing a bond issue. There is so much to do in the school that no matter how a teacher or counselor's job is restructured, there will always be more to do than a conscientious professional can do in the allotted time. But there often is very much that the principal can do to rearrange time so that it better serves the needs of the people in the school. As the major custodian of the school schedule, the principal should closely monitor its impact on the humans in the school and be ready to look to alternatives that will make the daily life of the school more pleasant for the people in it.

As a servant-leader perhaps the greatest service that you can perform is to keep the vision for the school. If you do not keep the vision, who will? A clear and compelling vision is how you can motivate others to accomplish outstanding things for all students. Vision is a target that rallies others and promotes a team spirit and willingness to go the extra mile to make a dream happen. All of us need something to look forward to. We need a challenge that is bigger than ourselves to drive us and energize us. If you, as principal, can inspire others through your vision and enthusiasm for the future, your staff will admire you and support a common or collective school vision. You must be so convinced that your vision is plausible, that you can persuade others of its merit and benefit for all children and youth. Every great work of art, architecture, or music started with a vision. Every victory in athletics started with a vision. Every successful math lesson started with a vision. Every effective school started with a vision. Winston Churchill's vision of victory over Hitler's powerful Nazi forces was the motivating force for his countrymen and, indeed, the world. While people listened to Churchill's eloquent and persuasive radio broadcasts after Luftwaffe bombs had destroyed much of London and other British cities, the people began to believe that they would prevail in spite of all the terror and fear. Joan of Arc had a vision to free her country from English domination and persuaded the Dauphin and others at Chinon to give her an army. Inspired by her vision and her devotion for her beloved France, Joan of Arc led her armies to stunning victories over the English. Visions can build magnificent cathedrals, win athletic events and wars. Visions can also turn mediocre schools into high performing, team-oriented, sensitive places where people enjoy working and learning together. Team building starts with visioning what can be.

A School Principal's Vision
By an Anonymous Principal

Sixteen years ago, I broke away from the science class to become a school principal. I recall that I wanted more money and more status, and, besides, I had been certified by a state university. I told myself at the time that I would still be a teacher and stay close to the kids. Somewhere along the way paperwork, regulations, board meetings, committees, and reform legislation took their toll; I lost my vision. I grew callused to the requests from teachers for smaller classes with fewer troublemakers. I forgot the exhaustion brought on by teaching, encouraging, prodding, and reprimanding students in warm, dusty classrooms. I lost the sensitivity that once led me to look for the pain in the eyes of a lonely child and try to help. In my quest for higher test scores and smoother waters, I ignored the magic that occurs between devoted teachers and eager students.

In the midst of counting daily attendance, checking the cooling system, writing memos, directing the United Way, and counting books, I forgot that teaching and learning and caring are the trinity of education. My zeal for keeping the roof on caused the foundation to crack. My zeal to be an efficient manager of things made me blind to my role in building lives. In my fight with board politics and community brush fires, my heart forgot the peace found in students helping each other.

Yes, I am a school principal. I have the power and knowledge to build a new world by creating schools that are exciting places to learn. I can work with teachers, students, board members, and community to open the doors of the world of opportunity for every child. It is not too late to recall why I entered education. I can still recapture the compassion and the intellectual energy that filled me that first year of teaching. My resolve is to once again place the inquiring faces of students in the center of each task I do. I will strive to empower teachers, parents, and students to help me plan a better school, a more caring community. This will be my vision. (Hoyle, 1990)

CONCLUSION

We started this book with a superintendent telling a principal, "Oh, don't be so sensitive!" The authors realize that being "sensitive" is easy to say but difficult to do. Being sensitive to insensitive people is no small challenge in a time of political correctness and the pressures of the proper words to use when addressing people with different ethnic, cultural, and language backgrounds. These differences make life richer and more fulfilling for all of us in the education profession. The more we know about difference, the better we can create a common dream for all of us. It remains a challenge for us to learn to appreciate difference and celebrate a nation that is trying to give all people an equal chance. Equality is far from a reality, but with sensitive school leaders continuing the conversations with all people in the community and by continuing to learn about different cultures and family traditions, equality will come closer for more people in time.

The authors hope that the suggestions in this book will add to your knowledge and skills to help you be more sensitive to the needs of your students, staff, and community. The seven key elements of interpersonal sensitivity in Chapter 1 are benchmarks to help you build a professional development plan on interpersonal sensitivity. Perhaps, in time, you will become more sensitive to your own insensitivities and become more patient and tolerant of others who have not worked to be sensitive leaders. Remember, the most successful leaders can tolerate mistakes in themselves and in others. To make a mistake is human, to make the same mistake twice is dumb. At the end of a long difficult day, a secretary came into her supervisor's office and began to apologize for an error she had made on an important report that was due the next morning. The sensitive supervisor listened intently while reaching in the desk for a pencil. Looking up into the eyes of the distraught secretary, the supervisor said, "See this pencil? It has two ends—one end for creating and one end for erasing mistakes." With that deeply sensitive remark, the secretary returned to correct the report and the bond between the two professionals grew stronger than ever.

Plan to use the following skill building activity with your staff. Good luck in your never-ending search for interpersonal sensitivity.

SKILL BUILDING ACTIVITY

"The School for all Children and Staff." (This exercise helps a faculty envision a school that provides total human services for all students.)

Activity: Future School. Divide faculty into groups of 5 from different grade levels and subject areas.

Resources: Selected articles from *The Futurist*, a journal published by the World Future Society, 4916 St. Elmo Ave., Bethesda, MD 20814. Two books, i.e., Hoyle, J. (1995). *Leadership and Futuring: Making Visions Happen*, Corwin Press; and Schlecty, P. (1993). *The School of the Future*. Jossey-Bass. Purchase a flip chart pad with easels and felt tip pens for each group.

Session 1: Future School—Part 1.
Task: Create a school of the future that includes complete human services for all students (i.e., healthcare, family services, etc.) Each group will begin by listing the kinds of skills, attributes, knowledge, and values that the faculty would like the students to have when they graduate from their school. The second step is to create the most appropriate learning experiences for teaching those desired attributes.
Time: 2½ hours.

Session 2: Future School—Part 2.
Task: Each group will render a drawing of their school on the flip chart pad. The drawing will include the shape and size of the facility, the learning areas, and external features (i.e., recreation, community agencies, etc.).
Time: 2 hours.

This school of the future exercise can provide the driving force to keep the faculty sensitive to their clients and focused on the target. It can encourage them to come together to discuss the next steps in making their dream happen. The extent to which the shared vision of the future school becomes a reality rests with the enthusiastic support of the superintendent, school board, and you, the school principal. The faculty will stay focused on the vision only if you constantly remain sensitive to their busy lives and continue to tell the dream over and over. You must be a constant source of encouragement. You are the "straw that stirs the drink" and remember, "you can't light a fire with a wet match" (Hoyle, 1995).

Your interpersonal sensitivity will continue to be visible and will help make you the kind of school leader you want to be if your visions are clear and greater than yourself. Leaders with vision stand far in front of the managers who keep a clean desk and expect order and tradition in "their" school. Visions can lead to disorder and confusion, but the journey to discovery for a better place for kids and staff can lead to enthusiasm for life and for education.

REFERENCES

Amundson, K. (1988). *Challenges for school leaders*. Arlington, VA: The American Association of School Administrators.

Baptise, P.H. (1988). "Multicultural education." In Gorton, R., Schneider, G., and Fisher, J. (eds.) *Encyclopedia of School Administration and Supervision*. Phoenix, AR: Oryx Press, 174–175.

Bolman, L., & Deal, T. (1993). *The Path to School Leadership*. Newbury Park, CA: Corwin Press, Inc.

Bradley, A. (1995, October 18). Assignment incomplete: The unfinished business of school reform. *Education Week*, 1, 13.

Bridges, E. (1967). A model for shared decision making in the school principalship. *Educational Administration Quarterly*, 3:49–61.

Chaffee, J., & Olds, R. (1979). *Champions of Children*. Arlington, VA: The American Association of School Administrators.

Charner, I., Fraser, B., Hubbard, S., Rogers, A., & Horne, R. (1995). Reforms of the school-to-work transition. *Phi Delta Kappan*, 77(1).

Clark, S. (1995, May). What leadership skills do principals really need? *The School Administrator*, 5(52):8–11.

Covey, S. (1990). *Principle-centered Leadership*. New York: Simon & Schuster.

Drucker, P. (1993). *Post-Capitalist Society*. New York: Harper Business.

Ehrmann, M. (1927). *Desiderata*. Boston, MA: Crescendo Publishing Co.

Elkind, D. (1995, September). School and family in the post-modern world. *Phi Delta Kappan*, 77(1):8–14.

Enoch, S. (1995, November). The dynamics of home-school relationships. *The School Administrator, 10*(52):24–27. Permission granted.

Epstein, J. (1995, May). School/family/community partnerships. *Phi Delta Kappan, 76*(9):701–712.

Frankl, V. (1967). *Man's Search for Meaning.* New York: Washington Square Publishing.

Getzels, J., & Guba, E. (1957). Social behavior and the administrative process. *School Review, 65*:423–441.

Gibbs, N. (1995). The EQ factor. *Time.* October 2; 60–68.

Glickman, C. (1990). Pushing school reform to a new edge: The seven ironies of school empowerment. *Phi Delta Kappan, 72*(1):68–75.

Glickman, C., & Pajak, E. (1983). "A cause beyond oneself." Synthesis Policy Paper, Southwest Development Laboratory. Austin, TX, 6(4).

Goleman, D. (1995). *Emotional Intelligence.* New York: Bantam Books Publishers.

Greer, J. (1995). The autonomous school. In Richardson, M., et al. (eds.), *School Empowerment.* Lancaster, PA: Technomic Publishing Co., Inc.

Homans, G. (1950). *The Human Group.* New York: Harcourt, Brace, and World, Inc.

Hoyle, J. (1994, January). Can a principal run the show and be a democratic leader? *Bulletin, 78*(558):33–40. Permission granted.

Hoyle, J. (1995). *Leadership and Futuring: Making Visions Happen.* Newbury, CA: Corwin Press Publishing Co., Inc.

Hoyle, J. (1992, November). Ten commandments for successful site-based management. *Bulletin, 76*(547):81–87. Permission granted. For more information about NASSA programs and/or services, call (703) 860-0200.

Hoyle, J., English, F., & Steffy, B. (1994). *Skills for Successful School Leaders.* Arlington, VA: The American Association of School Administrators.

Hoyle, J. (1990, March). "A school administrator's vision." *The School Administrator*. American Association of School Administrators. An adaptation.

Knapp, M. (1995). How shall we study comprehensive collaborative services for children and families? *Educational Researcher*, 24(4):5–16.

Kozol, J. (1995). *Amazing grace*. New York: Crown Publishers, Inc.

Lachmann, L., & Taylor, L. (1995). *Schools for All*. Albany, NY: Delmar Publishers.

Luft, J. (1984). *Group Processes: An Introduction to Group Dynamics*. Palo Alto, CA: Mayfield Publishing Company.

Meyers, C., & Meyers, L. (1995). *The Professional Educator*. Albany, NY: Wadsworth Publishing Co.

Mehrabien, A. (1971). *Silent Messages*. Belmont, CA: Wadsworth.

Muck, P. (1995). Fort Bend puts parents to work helping pupils. Houston, TX: *Houston Chronicle*. Sunday, Dec. 10; 37, 46, 47.

Muse, I., Sperry, D., Voelker, M., Harrington, P., & Harris, D. (1993). Interpersonal sensitivity. In Thomson, S. (ed.) *Principals for Our Changing Schools*. Fairfax, VA: National Policy Board for Educational Administration, 1–23.

Parsley, J. (1991). Reshaping student learning. *The School Administrator*, 7(48):9, 11, 13, 14.

Restine, N. (1995). Foreword. In Richardson, M., Lane, K., and Flanigan, J. (1995). *School empowerment*. Lancaster, PA: Technomic Publishing Co., Inc.

Stratton, J. (1995). *How students have changed*. Arlington, VA: The American Association of School Administrators.

Thomson, S. (Ed.). (1993). *Principals for Our Changing Schools*. Fairfax, VA: National Policy Board of Educational Administration.

Thomson, S. (1990). New framework for preparing principals developed by the National Commission for the Principals. News Release. Fairfax, VA: National Commission for the Principalship.

Weld, B. (1987). *Upper Room, 53*(2) (June).
Woestandiek, A. (1995, October 12). *The Houston Chronicle.* 7a.